Marriage

Vol III

Herbert George Wells

BOOK THE THIRD

MARJORIE AT LONELY HUT

CHAPTER THE FIRST

Successes

§ 1

I find it hard to trace the accumulation of moods and feelings that led Trafford and Marjorie at last to make their extraordinary raid upon Labrador. In a week more things happen in the thoughts of such a man as Trafford, changes, revocations, deflections, than one can chronicle in the longest of novels. I have already in an earlier passage of this story sought to give an image of the confused content of a modern human mind, but that pool was to represent a girl of twenty, and Trafford now was a man of nearly thirty-five, and touching life at a hundred points for one of the undergraduate Marjorie's. Perhaps that made him less confused, but it certainly made him fuller. Let me attempt therefore only the broad outline of his changes of purpose and activity until I come to the crucial mood that made these two lives a little worth telling about, amidst the many thousands of such lives that people are living to-day....

It took him seven years from his conclusive agreement with Solomonson to become a rich and influential man. It took him only seven years, because already by the mere accidents of intellectual interest he was in possession of knowledge of the very greatest economic importance, and because Solomonson was full of that practical loyalty and honesty that distinguishes his race. I think that in any case Trafford's vigor and subtlety of mind would have achieved the prosperity he had found necessary to himself, but it might have been, under less favorable auspices, a much longer and more tortuous struggle. Success and security were never so abundant nor so easily attained by men with capacity and a sense of proportion as they are in the varied and flexible world of to-day. We live in an affluent age with a nearly incredible continuous fresh increment of power pouring in from mechanical invention, and compared with our own, most other periods have been meagre and anxious and hard-up times. Our problems are constantly less the problems of submission and consolation and continually more problems of opportunity....

Trafford found the opening campaign, the operation with the plantation shares and his explosion of Behrens' pretensions extremely uncongenial. It left upon his mind a confused series of memories of interviews and talks in offices for the most part dingy and slovenly, of bales of press-cuttings and blue-pencilled financial publications, of unpleasing encounters with a number of bright-eyed, flushed, excitable and extremely cunning men, of having to be reserved and limited in his talk upon all occasions, and of all the worst aspects of Solomonson. All that part of the new treatment of life that was to make him rich gave him sensations as though he had ceased to wash himself mentally, until he regretted his old life in his laboratory as a traveller in a crowded night train among filthy people might regret the bathroom he had left behind him....

But the development of his manufacture of rubber was an entirely different business, and for a time profoundly interesting. It took him into a new astonishing world, the world of large-scale manufacture and industrial organization. The actual planning of the works was not in itself anything essentially new to him. So far as all that went it was scarcely more than the problem of arranging an experiment upon a huge and permanent scale, and all that quick ingenuity, that freshness and directness of mind that had made his purely scientific work so admirable had ample and agreeable scope. Even the importance of cost and economy at every point in the process involved no system of considerations that was altogether novel to him. The British investigator knows only too well the necessity for husbanded material and inexpensive substitutes. But strange factors came in, a new region of interest was opened with the fact that instead of one experimenter working with the alert responsive assistance of Durgan, a multitude of human beings—even in the first drafts of his project they numbered already two hundred, before the handling and packing could be considered—had to watch, control, assist or perform every stage in a long elaborate synthesis. For the first time in his life Trafford encountered the reality of Labour, as it is known to the modern producer.

It will be difficult in the future, when things now subtly or widely separated have been brought together by the receding perspectives of time, for the historian to realize just how completely out of the thoughts of such a young man as Trafford the millions of people who live and die in organized productive industry had been. That vast world of toil and weekly anxiety, ill-trained and stupidly directed effort and mental and moral feebleness, had been as much beyond the living circle of his experience as the hosts of Genghis Khan or the social life of the Forbidden City. Consider the limitations of his world. In all his life hitherto he had never been beyond a certain prescribed area of London's immensities, except by the most casual and uninstructive straying. He knew

Chelsea and Kensington and the north bank and (as a boy) Battersea Park, and all the strip between Kensington and Charing Cross, with some scraps of the Strand as far as the Law Courts, a shop or so in Tottenham Court Road and fragments about the British Museum and Holborn and Regent's Park, a range up Edgware Road to Maida Vale, the routes west and south-west through Uxbridge and Putney to the country, and Wimbledon Common and Putney Heath. He had never been on Hampstead Heath nor visited the Botanical Gardens nor gone down the Thames below London Bridge, nor seen Sydenham nor Epping Forest nor the Victoria Park. Take a map and blot all he knew and see how vast is the area left untouched. All industrial London, all wholesale London, great oceans of human beings fall into that excluded area. The homes he knew were comfortable homes, the poor he knew were the parasitic and dependent poor of the West, the shops, good retail shops, the factories for the most part engaged in dressmaking.

Of course he had been informed about this vast rest of London. He knew that as a matter of fact it existed, was populous, portentous, puzzling. He had heard of "slums," read "Tales of Mean Streets," and marvelled in a shallow transitory way at such wide wildernesses of life, apparently supported by nothing at all in a state of grey, darkling but prolific discomfort. Like the princess who wondered why the people having no bread did not eat cake, he could never clearly understand why the population remained there, did not migrate to more attractive surroundings. He had discussed the problems of those wildernesses as young men do, rather confidently, very ignorantly, had dismissed them, recurred to them, and forgotten them amidst a press of other interests, but now it all suddenly became real to him with the intensity of a startling and intimate contact. He discovered this limitless, unknown, greater London, this London of the majority, as if he had never thought of it before. He went out to inspect favourable sites in regions whose very names were unfamiliar to him, travelled on dirty little intraurban railway lines to hitherto unimagined railway stations, found parks, churches, workhouses, institutions, public-houses, canals, factories, gas-works, warehouses, foundries and sidings, amidst a multitudinous dinginess of mean houses, shabby back-yards, and ill-kept streets. There seemed to be no limits to this threadbare side of London, it went on northward, eastward, and over the Thames southward, for mile after mile—endlessly. The factories and so forth clustered in lines and banks upon the means of communication, the homes stretched between, and infinitude of parallelograms of grimy boxes with public-houses at the corners and churches and chapels in odd places, towering over which rose the council schools, big, blunt, truncated-looking masses, the means to an education as blunt and truncated, born of tradition and confused purposes, achieving by accident what they achieve at all.

And about this sordid-looking wilderness went a population that seemed at first as sordid. It was in no sense a tragic population. But it saw little of the sun, felt the wind but rarely, and so had a white, dull skin that looked degenerate and ominous to a West-end eye. It was not naked nor barefooted, but it wore cheap clothes that were tawdry when new, and speedily became faded, discoloured, dusty, and draggled. It was slovenly and almost wilfully ugly in its speech and gestures. And the food it ate was rough and coarse if abundant, the eggs it consumed "tasted"—everything "tasted"; its milk, its beer, its bread was degraded by base adulterations, its meat was hacked red stuff that hung in the dusty air until it was sold; east of the city Trafford could find no place where by his standards he could get a tolerable meal tolerably served. The entertainment of this eastern London was jingle, its religion clap-trap, its reading feeble and sensational rubbish without kindliness or breadth. And if this great industrial multitude was neither tortured nor driven nor cruelly treated—as the slaves and common people of other days have been—yet it was universally anxious, perpetually anxious about urgent small necessities and petty dissatisfying things....

That was the general effect of this new region in which he had sought out and found the fortunate site for his manufacture of rubber, and against this background it was that he had now to encounter a crowd of selected individuals, and weld them into a harmonious and successful "process." They came out from their millions to him, dingy, clumsy, and at first it seemed without any individuality. Insensibly they took on character, rounded off by unaccustomed methods into persons as marked and distinctive as any he had known.

There was Dowd, for instance, the technical assistant, whom he came to call in his private thoughts Dowd the Disinherited. Dowd had seemed a rather awkward, potentially insubordinate young man of unaccountably extensive and curiously limited attainments. He had begun his career in a crowded home behind and above a baker's shop in Hoxton, he had gone as a boy into the works of a Clerkenwell electric engineer, and there he had developed that craving for knowledge which is so common in poor men of the energetic type. He had gone to classes, read with a sort of fury, feeding his mind on the cheap and adulterated instruction of grant-earning crammers and on stale, meretricious and ill-chosen books; his mental food indeed was the exact parallel of the rough, abundant, cheap and nasty groceries and meat that gave the East-ender his spots and dyspeptic complexion, the cheap text-books were like canned meat and dangerous with intellectual ptomaines, the rascally encyclopædias like weak and whitened bread, and Dowd's mental complexion, too, was leaden and spotted. Yet essentially he wasn't, Trafford found, by any means bad stuff; where his knowledge had had a chance of touching reality it became admirable, and he was full of energy in his work and a sort of honest zeal about the things of the mind. The two men grew from an acute mutual criticism into a mutual respect.

At first it seemed to Trafford that when he met Dowd he was only meeting Dowd, but a time came when it seemed to him that in meeting Dowd he was meeting all that vast new England outside the range of ruling-class dreams, that multitudinous greater England, cheaply treated, rather out of health, angry, energetic and now becoming intelligent and critical, that England which organized industrialism has created. There were nights when he thought for hours about Dowd. Other figures grouped themselves round him—Markham, the head clerk, the quintessence of East-end respectability, who saw to the packing; Miss Peckover, an ex-telegraph operator, a woman so entirely reliable and unobservant that the most betraying phase of the secret process could be confidently entrusted to her hands. Behind them were clerks, workmen, motor-van men, work-girls, a crowd of wage-earners, from amidst which some individual would assume temporary importance and interest by doing something wrong, getting into trouble, becoming insubordinate, and having contributed a little vivid story to Trafford's gathering impressions of life, drop back again into undistinguished subordination.

Dowd became at last entirely representative.

When first Trafford looked Dowd in the eye, he met something of the hostile interest one might encounter in a swordsman ready to begin a duel. There was a watchfulness, an immense reserve. They discussed the work and the terms of their relationship, and all the while Trafford felt there was something almost threateningly not mentioned.

Presently he learnt from a Silvertown employer what that concealed aspect was. Dowd was "that sort of man who makes trouble," disposed to strike rather than not upon a grievance, with a taste for open-air meetings, a member, obstinately adherent in spite of friendly remonstrance, of the Social Democratic Party. This in spite of his clear duty to a wife and two small white knobby children. For a time he would not talk to Trafford of anything but business—Trafford was so manifestly the enemy, not to be trusted, the adventurous plutocrat, the exploiter—when at last Dowd did open out he did so defiantly, throwing opinions at Trafford as a mob might hurl bricks at windows. At last they achieved a sort of friendship and understanding, an amiability as it were, in hostility, but never from first to last would he talk to Trafford as one gentleman to another; between them, and crossed only by flimsy, temporary bridges, was his sense of incurable grievances and fundamental injustice. He seemed incapable of forgetting the disadvantages of his birth and upbringing, the inferiority and disorder of the house that sheltered him, the poor food that nourished him, the deadened air he breathed, the limited leisure, the inadequate books. Implicit in his every word and act was the assurance that but for this handicap he could have filled Trafford's place, while Trafford would certainly have failed in his.

For all these things Dowd made Trafford responsible; he held him to that inexorably.

"You sweat us," he said, speaking between his teeth; "you limit us, you stifle us, and away there in the West-end, you and the women you keep waste the plunder."

Trafford attempted palliation. "After all," he said, "it's not me so particularly——"

"But it is," said Dowd.

"It's the system things go upon."

"You're the responsible part of it. You have freedom, you have power and endless opportunity—"

Trafford shrugged his shoulders.

"It's because your sort wants too much," said Dowd, "that my sort hasn't enough."

"Tell me how to organize things better."

"Much you'd care. They'll organize themselves. Everything is drifting to class separation, the growing discontent, the growing hardship of the masses.... Then you'll see."

"Then what's going to happen?"

"Overthrow. And social democracy."

"How is that going to work?"

Dowd had been cornered by that before. "I don't care if it doesn't work," he snarled, "so long as we smash up this. We're getting too sick to care what comes after."

"Dowd," said Trafford abruptly, "I'm not so satisfied with things."

Dowd looked at him askance. "You'll get reconciled to it," he said. "It's ugly here—but it's all right there—at the spending end.... Your sort has got to grab, your sort has got to spend—until the thing works out and the social revolution makes an end of you."

"And then?"

Dowd became busy with his work.

Trafford stuck his hands in his pockets and stared out of the dingy factory window.

"I don't object so much to your diagnosis," he said, "as to your remedy. It doesn't strike me as a remedy."

"It's an end," said Dowd, "anyhow. My God! When I think of all the women and shirkers flaunting and frittering away there in the West, while here men and women toil and worry and starve...." He stopped short like one who feels too full for controlled speech.

"Dowd," said Trafford after a fair pause, "What would you do if you were me?"

"Do?" said Dowd.

"Yes," said Trafford as one who reconsiders it, "what would you do?"

"Now that's a curious question, Mr. Trafford," said Dowd, turning to regard him. "Meaning—if I were in your place?"

"Yes," said Trafford. "What would you do in my place?"

"I should sell out of this place jolly quick," he said.

"Sell!" said Trafford softly.

"Yes—sell. And start a socialist daily right off. An absolutely independent, unbiassed socialist daily."

"And what would that do?"

"It would stir people up. Every day it would stir people up."

"But you see I can't edit. I haven't the money for half a year of a socialist daily.... And meanwhile people want rubber."

Dowd shook his head. "You mean that you and your wife want to have the spending of six or eight thousand a year," he said.

"I don't make half of that," said Trafford.

"Well—half of that," pressed Dowd. "It's all the same to me."

Trafford reflected. "The point where I don't agree with you," he said, "is in supposing that my scale of living—over there, is directly connected with the scale of living—about here."

"Well, isn't it?"

"'Directly,' I said. No. If we just stopped it—over there—there'd be no improvement here. In fact, for a time it would mean dislocations. It might mean permanent, hopeless, catastrophic dislocation. You know that as well as I do. Suppose the West-end became—Tolstoyan; the East would become chaos."

"Not much likelihood," sneered Dowd.

"That's another question. That we earn together here and that I spend alone over there, it's unjust and bad, but it isn't a thing that admits of any simple remedy. Where we differ, Dowd, is about that remedy. I admit the disease as fully as you do. I, as much as you, want to see the dawn of a great change in the ways of human living. But I don't think the diagnosis is complete and satisfactory; our problem is an intricate muddle of disorders, not one simple disorder, and I don't see what treatment is indicated."

"Socialism," said Dowd, "is indicated."

"You might as well say that health is indicated," said Trafford with a note of impatience in his voice. "Does any one question that if we could have this socialist state in which every one is devoted and every one is free, in which there is no waste and no want, and beauty and brotherhood prevail universally, we wouldn't? But——. You socialists have no scheme of government, no scheme of economic organization, no intelligible guarantees of personal liberty, no method of progress, no ideas about marriage, no plan—except those little pickpocket plans of the Fabians that you despise as much as I do—for making this order into that other order you've never yet taken the trouble to work out even in principle. Really you know, Dowd, what is the good of pointing at my wife's dresses and waving the red flag at me, and talking of human miseries——"

"It seems to wake you up a bit," said Dowd with characteristic irrelevance.

§ 2

The accusing finger of Dowd followed Trafford into his dreams.

Behind it was his grey-toned, intelligent, resentful face, his smouldering eyes, his slightly frayed collar and vivid, ill-chosen tie. At times Trafford could almost hear his flat insistent voice, his measured h-less speech. Dowd was so penetratingly right,—and so ignorant of certain essentials, so wrong in his forecasts and ultimates. It was true beyond disputing that Trafford as compared with Dowd had opportunity, power of a sort, the prospect and possibility of leisure. He admitted the liability that followed on that advantage. It expressed so entirely the spirit of his training that with Trafford the noble maxim of the older socialists; "from each according to his ability, to each according to his need," received an intuitive acquiescence. He had no more doubt than Dowd that Dowd was the victim of a subtle evasive injustice, innocently and helplessly underbred, underfed, cramped and crippled, and that all his own surplus made him in a sense Dowd's debtor.

But Dowd's remedies!

Trafford made himself familiar with the socialist and labor newspapers, and he was as much impressed by their honest resentments and their enthusiastic hopefulness as he was repelled by their haste and ignorance, their cocksure confidence in untried reforms and impudent teachers, their indiscriminating progressiveness, their impulsive lapses into hatred, misrepresentation and vehement personal abuse. He was in no mood for the humours of human character, and he found the ill-masked feuds and jealousies of the leaders, the sham statecraft of G. B. Magdeberg, M.P., the sham

Machiavellism of Dorvil, the sham persistent good-heartedness of Will Pipes, discouraging and irritating. Altogether it seemed to him the conscious popular movement in politics, both in and out of Parliament, was a mere formless and indeterminate aspiration. It was a confused part of the general confusion, symptomatic perhaps, but exercising no controls and no direction.

His attention passed from the consideration of this completely revolutionary party to the general field of social reform. With the naïve directness of a scientific man, he got together the published literature of half a dozen flourishing agitations and philanthropies, interviewed prominent and rather embarrassed personages, attended meetings, and when he found the speeches too tiresome to follow watched the audience about him. He even looked up Aunt Plessington's Movement, and filled her with wild hopes and premature boastings about a promising convert. "Marjorie's brought him round at last!" said Aunt Plessington. "I knew I could trust my little Madge!" His impression was not the cynic's impression of these wide shallows of activity. Progress and social reform are not, he saw, mere cloaks of hypocrisy; a wealth of good intention lies behind them in spite of their manifest futility. There is much dishonesty due to the blundering desire for consistency in people of hasty intention, much artless and a little calculated self-seeking, but far more vanity and amiable feebleness of mind in their general attainment of failure. The Plessingtons struck him as being after all very typical of the publicist at large, quite devoted, very industrious, extremely presumptuous and essentially thin-witted. They would cheat like ill-bred children for example, on some petty point of reputation, but they could be trusted to expend, ineffectually indeed, but with the extremest technical integrity, whatever sums of money their adherents could get together....

He emerged from this inquiry into the proposed remedies and palliatives for Dowd's wrongs with a better opinion of people's hearts and a worse one of their heads than he had hitherto entertained.

Pursuing this line of thought he passed from the politicians and practical workers to the economists and sociologists. He spent the entire leisure of the second summer after the establishment of the factory upon sociological and economic literature. At the end of that bout of reading he attained a vivid realization of the garrulous badness that rules in this field of work, and the prevailing slovenliness and negligence in regard to it. He chanced one day to look up the article on Socialism in the new Encyclopædia Britannica, and found in its entire failure to state the case for or against modern

Socialism, to trace its origins, or to indicate any rational development in the movement, a symptom of the universal laxity of interest in these matters. Indeed, the writer did not appear to have heard of modern Socialism at all; he discussed collective and individualist methods very much as a rather ill-read schoolgirl in a hurry for her college debating society might have done. Compared with the treatment of engineering or biological science in the same compilation, this article became almost symbolical of the prevailing habitual incompetence with which all this system of questions is still handled. The sciences were done scantily and carelessly enough, but they admitted at any rate the possibility of completeness; this did not even pretend to thoroughness.

One might think such things had no practical significance. And at the back of it all was Dowd, remarkably more impatient each year, confessing the failure of parliamentary methods, of trades unionism, hinting more and more plainly at the advent of a permanent guerilla war against capital, at the general strike and sabotage.

"It's coming to that," said Dowd; "it's coming to that."

"What's the good of it?" he said, echoing Trafford's words. "It's a sort of relief to the feelings. Why shouldn't we?"

§ 3

But you must not suppose that at any time these huge grey problems of our social foundations and the riddle of intellectual confusion one reaches through them, and the yet broader riddles of human purpose that open beyond, constitute the whole of Trafford's life during this time. When he came back to Marjorie and his home, a curtain of unreality fell between him and all these things. It was as if he stepped through such boundaries as Alice passed to reach her Wonderland; the other world became a dream again; as if he closed the pages of a vivid book and turned to things about him. Or again it was as if he drew down the blind of a window that gave upon a landscape, grave, darkling, ominous, and faced the warm realities of a brightly illuminated room....

In a year or so he had the works so smoothly organized and Dowd so reconciled, trained and encouraged that his own daily presence was unnecessary, and he would go only three and then only two mornings a week to conduct those secret phases in the preparation of his catalytic that even Dowd could not be trusted to know. He reverted more and more completely to his own proper world.

And the first shock of discovering that greater London which "isn't in it" passed away by imperceptible degrees. Things that had been as vivid and startling as new wounds became unstimulating and ineffective with repetition. He got used to the change from Belgravia to East Ham, from East Ham to Belgravia. He fell in with the unusual persuasion in Belgravia, that, given a firm and prompt Home Secretary, East Ham could be trusted to go on—for quite a long time anyhow. One cannot sit down for all one's life in the face of insoluble problems. He had a motor-car now that far outshone Magnet's, and he made the transit from west to east in the minimum of time and with the minimum of friction. It ceased to be more disconcerting that he should have workers whom he could dismiss at a week's notice to want or prostitution than that he should have a servant waiting behind his chair. Things were so. The main current of his life—and the main current of his life flowed through Marjorie and his home—carried him on. Rubber was his, but there were still limitless worlds to conquer. He began to take up, working under circumstances of considerable secrecy at Solomonson's laboratories at Riplings, to which he would now go by motor-car for two or three days at a time, the possibility of a cheap, resilient and very tough substance, rubber glass, that was to be, Solomonson was assured, the road surface of the future.

§ 4

The confidence of Solomonson had made it impossible for Trafford to alter his style of living almost directly upon the conclusion of their agreement. He went back to Marjorie to broach a financially emancipated phase. They took a furnished house at Shackleford, near Godalming in Surrey, and there they lived for nearly a year—using their Chelsea home only as a town apartment for Trafford when business held him in London. And there it was, in the pretty Surrey country, with the sweet air of pine and heather in Marjorie's blood, that their second child was born. It was a sturdy little boy, whose only danger in life seemed to be the superfluous energy with which he resented its slightest disrespect of his small but important requirements.

When it was time for Marjorie to return to London, spring had come round again, and Trafford's conceptions of life were adapting themselves to the new scale upon which they were now to do things. While he was busy creating his factory in the East End, Marjorie was displaying an equal if a less original constructive energy in Sussex Square, near Lancaster Gate, for there it was the new home was to be established. She set herself to furnish and arrange it so as to produce the maximum of surprise and chagrin in Daphne, and she succeeded admirably. The Magnets now occupied a flat in Whitehall Court, the furniture Magnet had insisted upon buying himself with all the occult cunning of the humorist in these matters, and not even Daphne could blind herself to the superiority both in arrangement and detail of Marjorie's home. That was very satisfactory, and so too was the inevitable exaggeration of Trafford's financial importance. "He can do what he likes in the rubber world," said Marjorie. "In Mincing Lane, where they deal in rubber shares, they used to call him and Sir Rupert the invaders; now they call them the Conquering Heroes.... Of course, it's mere child's play to Godwin, but, as he said, 'We want money.' It won't really interfere with his more important interests...."

I do not know why both those sisters were more vulgarly competitive with each other than with any one else; I have merely to record the fact that they were so.

The effect upon the rest of Marjorie's family was equally gratifying. Mr. Pope came to the house-warming as though he had never had the slightest objection to Trafford's antecedents, and told him casually after dinner that Marjorie had always been his favourite daughter, and that from the first he had expected great things of her. He told Magnet, who was the third man of the party, that he only hoped Syd and Rom would do as well as their elder sisters. Afterwards, in the drawing-room, he whacked Marjorie suddenly and very startlingly on the shoulder-blade—it was the first bruise he had given her since Buryhamstreet days. "You've made a man of him, Maggots," he said.

The quiet smile of the Christian Scientist was becoming now the fixed expression of Mrs. Pope's face, and it scarcely relaxed for a moment as she surveyed her daughter's splendours. She had triumphantly refused to worry over a rather serious speculative disappointment, but her faith in her prophet's spiritual power had been strengthened rather than weakened by the manifest insufficiency of his financial prestidigitations, and she was getting through life quite radiantly now, smiling at (but not, of course, giving way to) beggars, smiling at toothaches and headaches, both her own and other people's, smiling away doubts, smiling away everything that bows the spirit of those who are still in the bonds of the flesh....

Afterwards the children came round, Syd and Rom now with skirts down and hair up, and rather stiff in the fine big rooms, and Theodore in a high collar and very anxious to get Trafford on his side in his ambition to chuck a proposed bank clerkship and go in for professional aviation....

It was pleasant to be respected by her family again, but the mind of Marjorie was soon reaching out to the more novel possibilities of her changed position. She need no longer confine herself to teas and afternoons. She could now, delightful thought! give dinners. Dinners are mere vulgarities for the vulgar, but in the measure of your brains does a dinner become a work of art. There is the happy blending of a modern and distinguished simplicity with a choice of items essentially good and delightful and just a little bit not what was expected. There is the still more interesting and difficult blending and arrangement of the diners. From the first Marjorie resolved on a round table, and the achievement of that rare and wonderful thing, general conversation. She had a clear centre, with a circle of silver bowls filled with short cut flowers and low shaded, old silver candlesticks adapted to the electric light. The first dinner was a nervous experience for her, but happily Trafford seemed unconscious of the importance of the occasion and talked very easily and well; at last she attained her old ambition to see Sir Roderick Dover in her house, and there was Remington, the editor of the Blue Weekly and his silent gracious wife; Edward Crampton, the historian, full of surprising new facts about Kosciusko; the Solomonsons and Mrs. Millingham, and Mary Gasthorne the novelist. It was a good talking lot. Remington sparred agreeably with the old Toryism of Dover, flank attacks upon them both were delivered by Mrs. Millingham and Trafford, Crampton instanced Hungarian parallels, and was happily averted by Mary Gasthorne with travel experiences in the Carpathians; the diamonds of Lady Solomonson and Mrs. Remington flashed and winked across the shining table, as their wearers listened with unmistakable intelligence, and when the ladies had gone upstairs Sir Rupert Solomonson told all the men exactly what he thought of the policy of the Blue Weekly, a balanced, common-sense judgment. Upstairs Lady Solomonson betrayed a passion of admiration for Mrs. Remington, and Mrs. Millingham mumbled depreciation of the same lady's intelligence in Mary Gasthorne's unwilling ear. "She's passive," said Mrs. Millingham. "She bores him...."

For a time Marjorie found dinner-giving delightful—it is like picking and arranging posies of human flowers—and fruits—and perhaps a little dried grass, and it was not long before she learnt that she was esteemed a success as a hostess. She gathered her earlier bunches in the Carmel and Solomonson circle, with a stiffening from among the literary and scientific friends of Trafford and his mother, and one or two casual and undervalued blossoms from Aunt Plessington's active promiscuities. She had soon a gaily flowering garden of her own to pick from. Its strength and finest display lay in its increasing proportion of political intellectuals, men in and about the House who relaxed their minds from the tense detailed alertness needed in political intrigues by conversation that rose at times to the level of the smarter sort of article in the half-crown reviews. The women were more difficult than the men, and Marjorie found herself wishing at times that girl novelists and playwrights were more abundant, or women writers on the average younger. These talked generally well, and one or two capable women of her own type talked and listened with an effect of talking; so many other women either chattered disturbingly, or else did not listen, with an effect of not talking at all, and so made gaps about the table. Many of these latter had to be asked because they belonged to the class of inevitable wives, sine-qua-nons, and through them she learnt the value of that priceless variety of kindly unselfish men who can create the illusion of attentive conversation in the most uncomfortable and suspicious natures without producing backwater and eddy in the general flow of talk.

Indisputably Marjorie's dinners were successful. Of course, the abundance and æsthetic achievements of Mrs. Lee still seemed to her immeasurably out of reach, but it was already possible to show Aunt Plessington how the thing ought really to be done, Aunt Plessington with her narrow, lank, austerely served table, with a sort of quarter-deck at her own end and a subjugated forecastle round Hubert. And accordingly the Plessingtons were invited and shown, and to a party, too, that restrained Aunt Plessington from her usual conversational prominence....

These opening years of Trafford's commercial phase were full of an engaging activity for Marjorie as for him, and for her far more completely than for him were the profounder solicitudes of life lost sight of in the bright succession of immediate events.

Marjorie did not let her social development interfere with her duty to society in the larger sense. Two years after the vigorous and resentful Godwin came a second son, and a year and a half later a third. "That's enough," said Marjorie, "now we've got to rear them." The nursery at Sussex Square had always been a show part of the house, but it became her crowning achievement. She had never forgotten the Lee display at Vevey, the shining splendours of modern maternity, the books, the apparatus, the space and light and air. The whole second floor was altered to accommodate these four triumphant beings, who absorbed the services of two nurses, a Swiss nursery governess and two housemaids—not to mention those several hundred obscure individuals who were yielding a sustaining profit in the East End. At any rate, they were very handsome and promising children, and little Margharita could talk three languages with a childish fluency, and invent and write a short fable in either French or German—with only as much misspelling as any child of eight may be permitted....

Then there sprang up a competition between Marjorie and the able, pretty wife of Halford Wallace, most promising of under-secretaries. They gave dinners against each other, they discovered young artists against each other, they went to first-nights and dressed against each other. Marjorie was ruddy and tall, Mrs. Halford Wallace dark and animated; Halford Wallace admired Marjorie, Trafford was insensible to Mrs. Halford Wallace. They played for points so vague that it was impossible for any one to say which was winning, but none the less they played like artists, for all they were worth....

Trafford's rapid prosperity and his implicit promise of still wider activities and successes brought him innumerable acquaintances and many friends. He joined two or three distinguished clubs, he derived an uncertain interest from a series of week-end visits to ample, good-mannered households, and for a time he found a distraction in little flashes of travel to countries that caught at his imagination, Morocco, Montenegro, Southern Russia.

I do not know whether Marjorie might not have been altogether happy during this early Sussex Square period, if it had not been for an unconquerable uncertainty about Trafford. But ever and again she became vaguely apprehensive of some perplexing unreality in her position. She had never had any such profundity of discontent as he experienced. It was nothing clear, nothing that actually penetrated, distressing her. It was at most an uneasiness. For him the whole fabric of life was, as it were, torn and pieced by a provocative sense of depths unplumbed that robbed it of all its satisfactions. For her these glimpses were as yet rare, mere moments of doubt that passed again and left her active and assured.

<h3 style="text-align:center">§ 5</h3>

It was only after they had been married six or seven years that Trafford began to realize how widely his attitudes to Marjorie varied. He emerged slowly from a naïve unconsciousness of his fluctuations,—a naïve unconsciousness of inconsistency that for most men and women remains throughout life. His ruling idea that she and he were friends, equals, confederates, knowing everything about each other, co-operating in everything, was very fixed and firm. But indeed that had become the remotest rendering of their relationship. Their lives were lives of intimate disengagement. They came nearest to fellowship in relation to their children; there they shared an immense common pride. Beyond that was a less confident appreciation of their common house and their joint effect. And then they liked and loved each other tremendously. They could play upon each other and please each other in a hundred different ways, and they did so, quite consciously, observing each other with the completest externality. She was still in many ways for him the bright girl he had admired in the examination, still the mysterious dignified transfiguration of that delightful creature on the tragically tender verge of motherhood; these memories were of more power with him than the present realities of her full-grown strength and capacity. He petted and played with the girl still; he was still tender and solicitous for that early woman. He admired and co-operated also with the capable, narrowly ambitious, beautiful lady into which Marjorie had developed, but those remoter experiences it was that gave the deeper emotions to their relationship.

The conflict of aims that had at last brought Trafford from scientific investigation into business, had left behind it a little scar of hostility. He felt his sacrifice. He felt that he had given something for her that she had had no right to exact, that he had gone beyond the free mutualities of honest love and paid a price for her; he had deflected the whole course of his life for her and he was entitled to repayments. Unconsciously he had become a slightly jealous husband. He resented inattentions and absences. He felt she ought to be with him and orient all her proceedings towards him. He did not like other people to show too marked an appreciation of her. She had a healthy love of admiration, and in addition her social ambitions made it almost inevitable that at times she should use her great personal charm to secure and retain adherents. He was ashamed to betray the resentments thus occasioned, and his silence widened the separation more than any protest could have done....

For his own part he gave her no cause for a reciprocal jealousy. Other women did not excite his imagination very greatly, and he had none of the ready disposition to lapse to other comforters which is so frequent a characteristic of the husband out of touch with his life's companion. He was perhaps an exceptional man in his steadfast loyalty to his wife. He had come to her as new to love as she had been. He had never in his life taken that one decisive illicit step which changes all the aspects of sexual life for a man even more than for a woman. Love for him was a thing solemn, simple, and unspoilt. He perceived that it was not so for most other men, but that did little to modify his own private attitude. In his curious scrutiny of the people about him, he did not fail to note the drift of adventures and infidelities that glimmers along beneath the even surface of our social life. One or two of his intimate friends, Solomonson was one of them, passed through "affairs." Once or twice those dim proceedings splashed upward to the surface in an open scandal. There came Remington's startling elopement with

Isabel Rivers, the writer, which took two brilliant and inspiring contemporaries suddenly and distressingly out of Trafford's world. Trafford felt none of that rage and forced and jealous contempt for the delinquents in these matters which is common in the ill-regulated, virtuous mind. Indeed, he was far more sympathetic with than hostile to the offenders. He had brains and imagination to appreciate the grim pathos of a process that begins as a hopeful quest, full of the suggestion of noble possibilities, full of the craving for missed intensities of fellowship and realization, that loiters involuntarily towards beauties and delights, and ends at last too often after gratification of an appetite, in artificially hideous exposures, and the pelting misrepresentations of the timidly well-behaved vile. But the general effect of pitiful evasions, of unavoidable meannesses, of draggled heroics and tortuously insincere explanations confirmed him in his aversion from this labyrinthine trouble of extraneous love....

But if Trafford was a faithful husband, he ceased to be a happy and confident one. There grew up in him a vast hinterland of thoughts and feelings, an accumulation of unspoken and largely of unformulated things in which his wife had no share. And it was in that hinterland that his essential self had its abiding place....

It came as a discovery; it remained for ever after a profoundly disturbing perplexity that he had talked to Marjorie most carelessly, easily and seriously, during their courtship and their honeymoon. He remembered their early intercourse now as an immense happy freedom in love. Then afterwards a curtain had fallen. That almost delirious sense of escaping from oneself, of having at last found some one from whom there need be no concealment, some one before whom one could stand naked-souled and assured of love as one stands before one's God, faded so that he scarce observed its passing, but only discovered at last that it had gone. He misunderstood and met misunderstanding. He found he could hurt her by the things he said, and be exquisitely hurt by her failure to apprehend the spirit of some ill-expressed intention. And it was so vitally important not to hurt, not to be hurt. At first he only perceived that he reserved himself; then there came the intimation of the question, was she also perhaps in such another hinterland as his, keeping herself from him?

He had perceived the cessation of that first bright outbreak of self-revelation, this relapse into the secrecies of individuality, quite early in their married life. I have already told of his first efforts to bridge their widening separation by walks and talks in the country, and by the long pilgrimage among the Alps that had ended so unexpectedly at Vevey. In the retrospect the years seemed punctuated with phases when "we must talk" dominated their intercourse, and each time the impulse of that recognized need passed away by insensible degrees again—with nothing said.

§ 6

Marjorie cherished an obstinate hope that Trafford would take up political questions and go into Parliament. It seemed to her that there was something about him altogether graver and wider than most of the active politicians she knew. She liked to think of those gravities assuming a practical form, of Trafford very rapidly and easily coming forward into a position of cardinal significance. It gave her general expenditure a quality of concentration without involving any uncongenial limitation to suppose it aimed at the preparation of a statesman's circle whenever Trafford chose to adopt that assumption. Little men in great positions came to her house and talked with opaque self-confidence at her table; she measured them against her husband while she played the admiring female disciple to their half-confidential talk. She felt that he could take up these questions and measures that they reduced to trite twaddle, open the wide relevancies behind them, and make them magically significant, sweep away the encrusting pettiness, the personalities and arbitrary prejudices. But why didn't he begin to do it? She threw out hints he seemed blind towards, she exercised miracles of patience while he ignored her baits. She came near intrigue in her endeavor to entangle him in political affairs. For a time it seemed to her that she was succeeding—I have already told of his phase of inquiry and interest in socio-political work—and then he relapsed into a scornful restlessness, and her hopes weakened again.

But he could not concentrate his mind, he could not think where to begin. Day followed day, each with its attacks upon his intention, its petty just claims, its attractive novelties of aspect. The telephone bell rang, the letters flopped into the hall, Malcom the butler seemed always at hand with some distracting oblong on his salver. Dowd was developing ideas for a reconstructed organization of the factory, Solomonson growing enthusiastic about rubber-glass, his house seemed full of women, Marjorie had an engagement for him to keep or the children were coming in to say good-night. To his irritated brain the whole scheme of his life presented itself at last as a tissue of interruptions which prevented his looking clearly at reality. More and more definitely he realized he wanted to get away and think. His former life of research became invested with an effect of immense dignity and of a steadfast singleness of purpose....

But Trafford was following his own lights, upon his own lines. He was returning to that faith in the supreme importance of thought and knowledge, upon which he had turned his back when he left pure research behind him. To that familiar end he came by an unfamiliar route, after his long, unsatisfying examination of social reform movements and social and political theories. Immaturity, haste and presumption vitiated all that region, and it seemed to him less and less disputable that the only escape for mankind from a continuing extravagant futility lay through the attainment of a quite unprecedented starkness and thoroughness of thinking about all these questions. This conception of a needed Renascence obsessed him more and more, and the persuasion, deeply felt if indistinctly apprehended, that somewhere in such an effort there was a part for him to play....

Life is too great for us or too petty. It gives us no tolerable middle way between baseness and greatness. We must die daily on the levels of ignoble compromise or perish tragically among the precipices. On the one hand is a life—unsatisfying and secure, a plane of dulled gratifications, mean advantages, petty triumphs, adaptations, acquiescences and submissions, and on the other a steep and terrible climb, set with sharp stones and bramble thickets and the possibilities of grotesque dislocations, and the snares of such temptation as comes only to those whose minds have been quickened by high desire, and the challenge of insoluble problems and the intimations of issues so complex and great, demanding such a nobility of purpose, such a steadfastness, alertness and openness of mind, that they fill the heart of man with despair....

There were moods when Trafford would, as people say, pull himself together, and struggle with his gnawing discontent. He would compare his lot with that of other men, reproach himself for a monstrous greed and ingratitude. He remonstrated with himself as one might remonstrate with a pampered child refusing to be entertained by a whole handsome nursery full of toys. Other men did their work in the world methodically and decently, did their duty by their friends and belongings, were manifestly patient through dullness, steadfastly cheerful, ready to meet vexations with a humorous smile, and grateful for orderly pleasures. Was he abnormal? Or was he in some unsuspected way unhealthy? Trafford neglected no possible explanations. Did he want this great Renascence of the human mind because he was suffering from some subtle form of indigestion? He invoked, independently of each other, the aid of two distinguished specialists. They both told him in exactly the same voice and with exactly the same air of guineas well earned: "What you want, Mr. Trafford, is a change."

Trafford brought his mind to bear upon the instances of contentment about him. He developed an opinion that all men and many women were potentially at least as restless as himself. A huge proportion of the usage and education in modern life struck upon him now as being a training in contentment. Or rather in keeping quiet and not upsetting things. The serious and responsible life of an ordinary prosperous man fulfilling the requirements of our social organization fatigues and neither completely satisfies nor completely occupies. Still less does the responsible part of the life of a woman of the prosperous classes engage all her energies or hold her imagination. And there has grown up a great informal organization of employments, games, ceremonies, social routines, travel, to consume these surplus powers and excessive cravings, which might otherwise change or shatter the whole order of human living. He began to understand the forced preoccupation with cricket and golf, the shooting, visiting, and so forth, to which the young people of the economically free classes in the community are trained. He discovered a theory for hobbies and specialized interests. He began to see why people go to Scotland to get away from London, and come to London to get away from Scotland, why they crowd to and fro along the Riviera, swarm over Switzerland, shoot, yacht, hunt, and maintain an immense apparatus of racing and motoring. Because so they are able to remain reasonably contented with the world as it is. He perceived, too, that a man who has missed or broken through the training to this kind of life, does not again very readily subdue himself to the security of these systematized distractions. His own upbringing had been antipathetic to any such adaptations; his years of research had given him the habit of naked intimacy with truth, filled him with a craving for reality and the destructive acids of a relentless critical method.

He began to understand something of the psychology of vice, to comprehend how small a part mere sensuality, how large a part the spirit of adventure and the craving for illegality, may play, in the career of those who are called evil livers. Mere animal impulses and curiosities it had always seemed possible to him to control, but now he was beginning to apprehend the power of that passion for escape, at any cost, in any way, from the petty, weakly stimulating, competitive motives of low-grade and law-abiding prosperity....

For a time Trafford made an earnest effort to adjust himself to the position in which he found himself, and make a working compromise with his disturbing forces. He tried to pick up the scientific preoccupation of his earlier years. He made extensive schemes, to Solomonson's great concern, whereby he might to a large extent disentangle himself from business. He began to hunt out forgotten note-books and yellowing sheets of memoranda. He found the resumption of research much more difficult than he had ever supposed possible. He went so far as to plan a laboratory, and to make some inquiries as to site and the cost of building, to the great satisfaction not only of Marjorie but of his mother. Old Mrs. Trafford had never expressed her concern at his abandonment of molecular physics for money-making, but now in her appreciation of his return to pure investigation she betrayed her sense of his departure.

But in his heart he felt that this methodical establishment of virtue by limitation would not suffice for him. He said no word of this scepticism as it grew in his mind. Marjorie was still under the impression that he was returning to research, and that she was free to contrive the steady preparation for that happier day when he should assume his political inheritance. And then presently a queer little dispute sprang up between them. Suddenly, for the first time since he took to business, Trafford found himself limiting her again. She was disposed, partly through the natural growth of her circle and her setting and partly through a movement on the part of Mrs. Halford Wallace, to move from Sussex Square into a larger, more picturesquely built house in a more central position. She particularly desired a good staircase. He met her intimations of this development with a curious and unusual irritation.

The idea of moving bothered him. He felt that exaggerated annoyance which is so often a concomitant of overwrought nerves. They had a dispute that was almost a quarrel, and though Marjorie dropped the matter for a time, he could feel she was still at work upon it.

Trafford Decides to Go

§ 1

A Haunting desire to go away into solitude grew upon Trafford very steadily. He wanted intensely to think, and London and Marjorie would not let him think. He wanted therefore to go away out of London and Marjorie's world. He wanted, he felt, to go away alone and face God, and clear things up in his mind. By imperceptible degrees this desire anticipated its realization. His activities were affected more and more by intimations of a determined crisis. One eventful day it seemed to him that his mind passed quite suddenly from desire to resolve. He found himself with a project, already broadly definite. Hitherto he hadn't been at all clear where he could go. From the first almost he had felt that this change he needed, the change by which he was to get out of the thickets of work and perplexity and distraction that held him captive, must be a physical as well as a mental removal; he must go somewhere, still and isolated, where sustained detached thinking was possible.... His preference, if he had one, inclined him to some solitude among the Himalaya Mountains. That came perhaps from Kim and the precedent of the Hindoo's religious retreat from the world. But this retreat he contemplated was a retreat that aimed at a return, a clarified and strengthened resumption of the world. And then suddenly, as if he had always intended it, Labrador flashed through his thoughts, like a familiar name that had been for a time quite unaccountably forgotten.

The word "Labrador" drifted to him one day from an adjacent table as he sat alone at lunch in the Liberal Union Club. Some bore was reciting the substance of a lecture to a fellow-member. "Seems to be a remarkable country," said the speaker. "Mineral wealth hardly glanced at, you know. Furs and a few score Indians. And at our doors. Practically—at our doors."

Trafford ceased to listen. His mind was taking up this idea of Labrador. He wondered why he had not thought of Labrador before.

He had two or three streams of thought flowing in his mind, as a man who muses alone is apt to do. Marjorie's desire to move had reappeared; a particular group of houses between Berkeley Square and Park Lane had taken hold of her fancy, she had urged the acquisition of one upon him that morning, and this kept coming up into consciousness like a wrong thread in a tapestry. Moreover, he was watching his fellow-members with a critical rather than a friendly eye. A half-speculative, half-hostile contemplation of his habitual associates was one of the queer aspects of this period of unsettlement. They exasperated him by their massive contentment with the surface of things. They came in one after another patting their ties, or pulling at the lapels of their coats, and looked about them for vacant places with a conscious ease of manner that irritated his nerves. No doubt they were all more or less successful and distinguished men, matter for conversation and food for anecdotes, but why did they trouble to give themselves the air of it? They halted or sat down by friends, enunciated vapid remarks in sonorous voices, and opened conversations in trite phrases, about London architecture, about the political situation or the morning's newspaper, conversations that ought, he felt, to have been thrown away unopened, so stale and needless they seemed to him. They were judges, lawyers of all sorts, bankers, company promoters, railway managers, stockbrokers, pressmen, politicians, men of leisure. He wondered if indeed they were as opaque as they seemed, wondered with the helpless wonder of a man of exceptional mental gifts whether any of them at any stage had had such thoughts as his, had wanted as acutely as he did now to get right out of the world. Did old Booch over there, for example, guzzling oysters, cry at times upon the unknown God in the vast silences of the night? But Booch, of course, was a member or something of the House of Laymen, and very sound on the thirty-nine articles—a man who ate oysters like that could swallow anything—and in the vast silences of the night he was probably heavily and noisily asleep....

Blenkins, the gentlemanly colleague of Denton in the control of the Old Country Gazette, appeared on his way to the pay-desk, gesticulating amiably en-route to any possible friend. Trafford returned his salutation, and pulled himself together immediately after in fear that he had scowled, for he hated to be churlish to any human being. Blenkins, too, it might be, had sorrow and remorse and periods of passionate self-distrust and self-examination; maybe Blenkins could weep salt tears, as Blenkins no doubt under suitable sword-play would reveal heart and viscera as quivering and oozy as any man's.

But to Trafford's jaundiced eyes just then, it seemed that if you slashed Blenkins across he would probably cut like a cheese....

Now, in Labrador——....

So soon as Blenkins had cleared, Trafford followed him to the pay-desk, and went on upstairs to the smoking-room, thinking of Labrador. Long ago he had read the story of Wallace and Hubbard in that wilderness.

There was much to be said for a winter in Labrador. It was cold, it was clear, infinitely lonely, with a keen edge of danger and hardship and never a letter or a paper.

One could provision a hut and sit wrapped in fur, watching the Northern Lights....

"I'm off to Labrador," said Trafford, and entered the smoking-room.

It was, after all, perfectly easy to go to Labrador. One had just to go....

As he pinched the end of his cigar, he became aware of Blenkins, with a gleam of golden glasses and a flapping white cuff, beckoning across the room to him. With that probable scowl on his conscience Trafford was moved to respond with an unreal warmth, and strolled across to Blenkins and a group of three or four other people, including that vigorous young politician, Weston Massinghay, and Hart, K.C., about the further fireplace. "We were talking of you," said Blenkins. "Come and sit down with us. Why don't you come into Parliament?"

"I've just arranged to go for some months to Labrador."

"Industrial development?" asked Blenkins, all alive.

"No. Holiday."

No Blenkins believes that sort of thing, but of course, if Trafford chose to keep his own counsel——

"Well, come into Parliament as soon as you get back."

Trafford had had that old conversation before. He pretended insensibility when Blenkins gestured to a vacant chair. "No," he said, still standing, "we settled all that. And now I'm up to my neck in—detail about Labrador. I shall be starting—before the month is out."

Blenkins and Hart simulated interest. "It's immoral," said Blenkins, "for a man of your standing to keep out of politics."

"It's more than immoral," said Hart; "it's American."

"Solomonson comes in to represent the firm," smiled Trafford, signalled the waiter for coffee, and presently disentangled himself from their company.

For Blenkins Trafford concealed an exquisite dislike and contempt; and Blenkins had a considerable admiration for Trafford, based on extensive misunderstandings. Blenkins admired Trafford because he was good-looking and well-dressed, with a beautiful and successful wife, because he had become reasonably rich very quickly and easily, was young and a Fellow of the Royal Society with a reputation that echoed in Berlin, and very perceptibly did not return Blenkins' admiration. All these things filled Blenkins with a desire for Trafford's intimacy, and to become the associate of the very promising political career that it seemed to him, in spite of Trafford's repudiations, was the natural next step in a deliberately and honourably planned life. He mistook Trafford's silences and detachment for the marks of a strong, silent man, who was scheming the immense, vulgar, distinguished-looking achievements that appeal to the Blenkins mind. Blenkins was a sentimentally loyal party Liberal, and as he said at times to Hart and Weston Massinghay: "If those other fellows get hold of him ——!"

Blenkins was the fine flower of Oxford Liberalism and the Tennysonian days. He wanted to be like King Arthur and Sir Galahad, with the merest touch of Launcelot, and to be perfectly upright and splendid and very, very successful. He was a fair, tenoring sort of person with an Arthurian moustache and a disposition to long frock coats. It had been said of him that he didn't dress like a gentleman, but that he dressed more like a gentleman than a gentleman ought to dress. It might have been added that he didn't behave like a gentleman, but that he behaved more like a gentleman than a gentleman ought to behave. He didn't think, but he talked and he wrote more thoughtfully in his leaders, and in the little dialogues he wrote in imitation of Sir Arthur Helps, than any other person who didn't think could possibly do. He was an orthodox Churchman, but very, very broad; he held all the doctrines, a distinguished sort of thing to do in an age of doubt, but there was a quality about them as he held them—as though they had been run over by something rather heavy. It was a flattened and slightly obliterated breadth—nothing was assertive, but nothing, under examination, proved to be altogether gone. His profuse thoughtfulness was not confined to his journalistic and literary work, it overflowed into Talks. He was a man for Great Talks, interminable rambling floods of boyish observation, emotional appreciation, and silly, sapient comment. He loved to discuss "Who are the Best Talkers now Alive?" He had written an essay, Talk in the Past. He boasted of week-ends when the Talk had gone on from the moment of meeting in the train to the moment of parting at Euston, or

Paddington, or Waterloo; and one or two hostesses with embittered memories could verify his boasting. He did his best to make the club a Talking Club, and loved to summon men to a growing circle of chairs....

Trafford had been involved in Talks on one or two occasions, and now, as he sat alone in the corridor and smoked and drank his coffee, he could imagine the Talk he had escaped, the Talk that was going on in the smoking room—the platitudes, the sagacities, the digressions, the sudden revelation of deep, irrational convictions. He reflected upon the various Talks at which he had assisted. His chief impression of them all was of an intolerable fluidity. Never once had he known a Talk thicken to adequate discussion; never had a new idea or a new view come to him in a Talk. He wondered why Blenkins and his like talked at all. Essentially they lived for pose, not for expression; they did not greatly desire to discover, make, or be; they wanted to seem and succeed. Talking perhaps was part of their pose of great intellectual activity, and Blenkins was fortunate to have an easy, unforced running of mind....

Over his cigar Trafford became profoundly philosophical about Talk. And after the manner of those who become profoundly philosophical he spread out the word beyond its original and proper intentions to all sorts of kindred and parallel things. Blenkins and his miscellany of friends in their circle of chairs were, after all, only a crude rendering of very much of intellectual activity of mankind. Men talked so often as dogs bark. Those Talkers never came to grips, fell away from topic to topic, pretended depth and evaded the devastating horrors of sincerity. Listening was a politeness amongst them that was presently rewarded with utterance. Tremendously like dogs they were, in a dog-fancying neighborhood on a summer week-day afternoon. Fluidity, excessive abundance, inconsecutiveness; these were the things that made Talk hateful to Trafford.

Wasn't most literature in the same class? Wasn't nearly all present philosophical and sociological discussion in the world merely a Blenkins circle on a colossal scale, with every one looming forward to get in a deeply thoughtful word edgeways at the first opportunity? Imagine any one in distress about his soul or about mankind, going to a professor of economics or sociology or philosophy! He thought of the endless, big, expensive, fruitless books, the windy expansions of industrious pedantry that mocked the spirit of inquiry. The fields of physical and biological science alone had been partially rescued from the floods of human inconsecutiveness. There at least a man must, on the whole, join on to the work of other men, stand a searching criticism, justify himself. Philosophically this was an age of relaxed schoolmen. He thought of Doctor Codger at Cambridge, bubbling away with his iridescent Hegelianism like a salted snail; of Doctor Quiller at Oxford, ignoring Bergson and fulminating a preposterous insular Pragmatism. Each contradicted the other fundamentally upon matters of universal concern; neither ever joined issue with the other. Why in the name of humanity didn't some one take hold of those two excellent gentlemen, and bang their busy heads together hard and frequently until they either compromised or cracked?

§ 2

He forgot these rambling speculations as he came out into the spring sunshine of Pall Mall, and halting for a moment on the topmost step, regarded the tidy pavements, the rare dignified shops, the waiting taxicabs, the pleasant, prosperous passers-by. His mind lapsed back to the thought that he meant to leave all this and go to Labrador. His mind went a step further, and reflected that he would not only go to Labrador, but—it was highly probable—come back again.

And then?

Why, after all, should he go to Labrador at all? Why shouldn't he make a supreme effort here?

Something entirely irrational within him told him with conclusive emphasis that he had to go to Labrador....

He remembered there was this confounded business of the proposed house in Mayfair to consider....

§ 3

It occurred to him that he would go a little out of his way, and look at the new great laboratories at the Romeike College, of which his old bottle-washer Durgan was, he knew, extravagantly proud. Romeike's widow was dead now and her will executed, and her substance half turned already to bricks and stone and glazed tiles and all those excesses of space and appliance which the rich and authoritative imagine must needs give us Science, however ill-selected and underpaid and slighted the users of those opportunities may be. The architects had had great fun with the bequest; a quarter of the site was devoted to a huge square surrounded by dignified, if functionless, colonnades, and adorned with those stone seats of honour which are always so chill and unsatisfactory as resting places in our island climate. The Laboratories, except that they were a little shaded by the colonnades, were everything a laboratory should be; the benches were miracles of convenience, there wasn't anything the industrious investigator might want, steam, high pressures, electric power, that he couldn't get by pressing a button or turning a switch, unless perhaps it was inspiring ideas. And the new library at the end, with its greys and greens, its logarithmic computators at every table, was a miracle of mental convenience.

Durgan showed his old professor the marvels.

"If he chooses to do something here," said Durgan not too hopefully, "a man can...."

"What's become of the little old room where we two used to work?" asked Trafford.

"They'll turn 'em all out presently," said Durgan, "when this part is ready, but just at present it's very much as you left it. There's been precious little research done there since you went away—not what I call research. Females chiefly—and boys. Playing at it. Making themselves into D.Sc.'s by a baby research instead of a man's examination. It's like broaching a thirty-two gallon cask full of Pap to think of it. Lord, sir, the swill! Research! Counting and weighing things! Professor Lake's all right, I suppose, but his work was mostly mathematical; he didn't do much of it here. No, the old days ended, sir, when you...."

He arrested himself, and obviously changed his words. "Got busy with other things."

Trafford surveyed the place; it seemed to him to have shrunken a little in the course of the three years that had intervened since he resigned his position. On the wall at the back there still hung, fly-blown and a little crumpled, an old table of constants he had made for his elasticity researches. Lake had kept it there, for Lake was a man of generous appreciations, and rather proud to follow in the footsteps of an investigator of Trafford's subtlety and vigor. The old sink in the corner where Trafford had once swilled his watch glasses and filled his beakers had been replaced by one of a more modern construction, and the combustion cupboard was unfamiliar, until Durgan pointed out that it had been enlarged. The ground-glass window at the east end showed still the marks of an explosion that had banished a clumsy student from this sanctuary at the very beginning of Trafford's career.

"By Jove!" he said after a silence, "but I did some good work here."

"You did, sir," said Durgan.

"I wonder—I may take it up again presently."

"I doubt it, sir," said Durgan.

"Oh! But suppose I come back?"

"I don't think you would find yourself coming back, sir," said Durgan after judicious consideration.

He adduced no shadow of a reason for his doubt, but some mysterious quality in his words carried conviction to Trafford's mind. He knew that he would never do anything worth doing in molecular physics again. He knew it now conclusively for the first time.

§ 4

He found himself presently in Bond Street. The bright May day had brought out great quantities of people, so that he had to come down from altitudes of abstraction to pick his way among them.

He was struck by the prevailing interest and contentment in the faces he passed. There was no sense of insecurity betrayed, no sense of the deeps and mysteries upon which our being floats like a film. They looked solid, they looked satisfied; surely never before in the history of the world has there been so great a multitude of secure-feeling, satisfied-looking, uninquiring people as there is to-day. All the tragic great things of life seem stupendously remote from them; pain is rare, death is out of sight, religion has shrunken to an inconsiderable, comfortable, reassuring appendage of the daily life. And with the bright small things of immediacy they are so active and alert. Never before has the world seen such multitudes, and a day must come when it will cease to see them for evermore.

As he shouldered his way through the throng before the Oxford Street shop windows he appreciated a queer effect, almost as it were of insanity, about all this rich and abundant and ultimately aimless life, this tremendous spawning and proliferation of uneventful humanity. These individual lives signified no doubt enormously to the individuals, but did all the shining, reflecting, changing existence that went by like bubbles in a stream, signify collectively anything more than the leaping, glittering confusion of shoaling mackerel on a sunlit afternoon? The pretty girl looking into the window schemed picturesque achievements with lace and ribbon, the beggar at the curb was alert for any sympathetic eye, the chauffeur on the waiting taxi-cab watched the twopences ticking on with a quiet satisfaction; each followed a keenly sought immediate end, but altogether? Where were they going altogether? Until he knew that, where was the sanity of statecraft, the excuse of any impersonal effort, the significance of anything beyond a life of appetites and self-seeking instincts?

He found that perplexing suspicion of priggishness affecting him again. Why couldn't he take the gift of life as it seemed these people took it? Why was he continually lapsing into these sombre, dimly religious questionings and doubts? Why after all should he concern himself with these riddles of some collective and ultimate meaning in things? Was he for all his ability and security so afraid of the accidents of life that on that account he clung to this conception of a larger impersonal issue which the world in general seemed to have abandoned so cheerfully? At any rate he did cling to it—and his sense of it made the abounding active life of this stirring, bristling thoroughfare an almost unendurable perplexity....

By the Marble Arch a little crowd had gathered at the pavement edge. He remarked other little knots towards Paddington, and then still others, and inquiring, found the King was presently to pass. They promised themselves the gratification of seeing the King go by. They would see a carriage, they would see horses and coachmen, perhaps even they might catch sight of a raised hat and a bowing figure. And this would be a gratification to them, it would irradiate the day with a sense of experiences, exceptional and precious. For that some of them had already been standing about for two or three hours.

He thought of these waiting people for a time, and then he fell into a speculation about the King. He wondered if the King ever lay awake at three o'clock in the morning and faced the riddle of the eternities or whether he did really take himself seriously and contentedly as being in himself the vital function of the State, performed his ceremonies, went hither and thither through a wilderness of gaping watchers, slept well on it. Was the man satisfied? Was he satisfied with his empire as it was and himself as he was, or did some vision, some high, ironical intimation of the latent and lost possibilities of his empire and of the world of Things Conceivable that lies beyond the poor tawdry splendours of our present loyalties, ever dawn upon him?

Trafford's imagination conjured up a sleepless King Emperor agonizing for humanity....

He turned to his right out of Lancaster Gate into Sussex Square, and came to a stop at the pavement edge.

From across the road he surveyed the wide white front and portals of the house that wasn't big enough for Marjorie.

§ 5

He let himself in with his latchkey.

Malcolm, his man, hovered at the foot of the staircase, and came forward for his hat and gloves and stick.

"Mrs. Trafford in?" asked Trafford.

"She said she would be in by four, sir."

Trafford glanced at his watch and went slowly upstairs.

On the landing there had been a rearrangement of the furniture, and he paused to survey it. The alterations had been made to accommodate a big cloisonné jar, that now glowed a wonder of white and tinted whites and luminous blues upon a dark, deep-shining stand. He noted now the curtain of the window had been changed from something—surely it had been a reddish curtain!—to a sharp clear blue with a black border, that reflected upon and sustained and encouraged the jar tremendously. And the wall behind—? Yes. Its deep brown was darkened to an absolute black behind the jar, and shaded up between the lacquer cabinets on either hand by insensible degrees to the general hue. It was wonderful, perfectly harmonious, and so subtly planned that it seemed it all might have grown, as flowers grow....

He entered the drawing-room and surveyed its long and handsome spaces. Post-impressionism was over and gone; three long pictures by young Rogerson and one of Redwood's gallant bronzes faced the tall windows between the white marble fireplaces at either end. There were two lean jars from India, a young boy's head from Florence, and in a great bowl in the remotest corner a radiant mass of azaleas....

His mood of wondering at familiar things was still upon him. It came to him as a thing absurd and incongruous that this should be his home. It was all wonderfully arranged into one dignified harmony, but he felt now that at a touch of social earthquake, with a mere momentary lapse towards disorder, it would degenerate altogether into litter, lie heaped together confessed the loot it was. He came to a stop opposite one of the Rogersons, a stiffly self-conscious shop girl in her Sunday clothes, a not unsuccessful emulation of Nicholson's wonderful Mrs. Stafford of Paradise Row. Regarded as so much brown and grey and amber-gold, it was coherent in Marjorie's design, but regarded as a work of art, as a piece of expression, how madly irrelevant was its humour and implications to that room and the purposes of that room! Rogerson wasn't perhaps trying to say much, but at any rate he was trying to say something, and Redwood too was asserting freedom and adventure, and the thought of that Florentine of the bust, and the patient, careful Indian potter, and every maker of all the little casual articles about him, produced an effect of muffled, stifled assertions. Against this subdued and disciplined background of muted, inarticulate cries,—cries for beauty, for delight, for freedom, Marjorie and her world moved and rustled and chattered and competed—wearing the skins of beasts, the love-plumage of birds, the woven cocoon cases of little silkworms....

"Preposterous," he whispered.

He went to the window and stared out; turned about and regarded the gracious variety of that long, well-lit room again, then strolled thoughtfully upstairs. He reached the door of his study, and a sound of voices from the schoolroom—it had recently been promoted from the rank of day nursery to this level—caught his mood. He changed his mind, crossed the landing, and was welcomed with shouts.

The rogues had been dressing up. Margharita, that child of the dreadful dawn, was now a sturdy and domineering girl of eight, and she was attired in a gilt paper mitre and her governess's white muslin blouse so tied at the wrists as to suggest long sleeves, a broad crimson band doing duty as a stole. She was Becket prepared for martyrdom at the foot of the altar. Godwin, his eldest son, was a hot-tempered, pretty-featured pleasantly self-conscious boy of nearly seven and very happy now in a white dragoon's helmet and rude but effective brown paper breastplate and greaves, as the party of assassin knights. A small acolyte in what was in all human probably one of the governess's more intimate linen garments assisted Becket, while the general congregation of Canterbury was represented by Edward, aged two, and the governess, disguised with a Union Jack tied over her head after the well-known fashion of the middle ages. After the children had welcomed their father and explained the bloody work in hand, they returned to it with solemn earnestness, while Trafford surveyed the tragedy. Godwin slew with admirable gusto, and I doubt if the actual Thomas of Canterbury showed half the stately dignity of Margharita.

The scene finished, they went on to the penance of Henry the Second; and there was a tremendous readjustment of costumes, with much consultation and secrecy. Trafford's eyes went from his offspring to the long, white-painted room, with its gay frieze of ships and gulls and its rug-variegated cork carpet of plain brick red. Everywhere it showed his wife's quick cleverness, the clean serviceable decorativeness of it all, the pretty patterned window curtains, the writing desks, the little library of books, the flowers and bulbs in glasses, the counting blocks and bricks and jolly toys, the blackboard on which the children learnt to draw in bold wide strokes, the big, well-chosen German colour prints upon the walls. And the children did credit to their casket; they were not only full of vitality but full of ideas, even Edward was already a person of conversation. They were good stuff anyhow....

It was fine in a sense, Trafford thought, to have given up his own motives and curiosities to afford this airy pleasantness of upbringing for them, and then came a qualifying thought. Would they in their turn for the sake of another generation have to give up fine occupations for mean occupations, deep thoughts for shallow? Would the world get them in turn? Would the girls be hustled and flattered into advantageous marriages, that dinners and drawing-rooms might still prevail? Would the boys, after this gracious beginning, presently have to swim submerged in another generation of Blenkinses and their Talk, toil in arduous self-seeking, observe, respect and manipulate shams, succeed or fail, and succeeding, beget amidst hope and beautiful emotions yet another generation doomed to insincerities and accommodations, and so die at last — as he must die?...

He heard his wife's clear voice in the hall below, and went down to meet her. She had gone into the drawing-room, and he followed her in and through the folding doors to the hinder part of the room, where she stood ready to open a small bureau. She turned at his approach, and smiled a pleasant, habitual smile....

She was no longer the slim, quick-moving girl who had come out of the world to him when he crawled from beneath the wreckage of Solomonson's plane, no longer the half-barbaric young beauty who had been revealed to him on the staircase of the Vevey villa. She was now a dignified, self-possessed woman, controlling her house and her life with a skilful, subtle appreciation of her every point and possibility. She was wearing now a simple walking dress of brownish fawn colour, and her hat was touched with a steely blue that made her blue eyes seem handsome and hard, and toned her hair to a merely warm brown. She had, as it were, subdued her fine colours into a sheath in order that she might presently draw them again with more effect.

"Hullo, old man!" she said, "you home?"

He nodded. "The club bored me—and I couldn't work."

Her voice had something of a challenge and defiance in it. "I've been looking at a house," she said. "Alice Carmel told me of it. It isn't in Berkeley Square, but it's near it. It's rather good."

He met her eye. "That's—premature," he said.

"We can't go on living in this one."

"I won't go to another."

"But why?"

"I just won't."

"It isn't the money?"

"No," said Trafford, with sudden fierce resentment. "I've overtaken you and beaten you there, Marjorie."

She stared at the harsh bitterness of his voice. She was about to speak when the door opened, and Malcom ushered in Aunt Plessington and Uncle Hubert. Husband and wife hung for a moment, and then realized their talk was at an end....

Marjorie went forward to greet her aunt, careless now of all that once stupendous Influence might think of her. She had long ceased to feel even the triumph of victory in her big house, her costly, dignified clothes, her assured and growing social importance. For five years Aunt Plessington had not even ventured to advise; had once or twice admired. All that business of Magnet was—even elaborately—forgotten....

Seven years of feverish self-assertion had left their mark upon both the Plessingtons. She was leaner, more gauntly untidy, more aggressively ill-dressed. She no longer dressed carelessly, she defied the world with her clothes, waved her tattered and dingy banners in its face. Uncle Hubert was no fatter, but in some queer way he had ceased to be thin. Like so many people whose peripheries defy the manifest quaint purpose of Providence, he was in a state of thwarted adiposity, and with all the disconnectedness and weak irritability characteristic of his condition. He had developed a number of nervous movements, chin-strokings, cheek-scratchings, and incredulous pawings at his more salient features.

"Isn't it a lark?" began Aunt Plessington, with something like a note of apprehension in her highpitched voice, and speaking almost from the doorway, "we're making a call together. I and Hubert! It's an attack in force."

Uncle Hubert goggled in the rear and stroked his chin, and tried to get together a sort of facial expression.

The Traffords made welcoming noises, and Marjorie advanced to meet her aunt.

"We want you to do something for us," said Aunt Plessington, taking two hands with two hands....

In the intervening years the Movement had had ups and downs; it had had a boom, which had ended abruptly in a complete loss of voice for Aunt Plessington—she had tried to run it on a patent non-stimulating food, and then it had entangled itself with a new cult of philanthropic theosophy from which it had been extracted with difficulty and in a damaged condition. It had never completely recovered from that unhappy association. Latterly Aunt Plessington had lost her nerve, and she had taken to making calls upon people with considerable and sometimes embarrassing demand for support, urging them to join committees, take chairs, stake reputations, speak and act as foils for her. If they refused she lost her temper very openly and frankly, and became industriously vindictive. She circulated scandals or created them. Her old assurance had deserted her; the strangulated contralto was losing its magic power, she felt, in this degenerating England it had ruled so long. In the last year or so she had become extremely snappy with Uncle Hubert. She ascribed much of the Movement's futility to the decline of his administrative powers and the increasing awkwardness of his gestures, and she did her utmost to keep him up to the mark. Her only method of keeping him up to the mark was to jerk the bit. She had now come to compel Marjorie to address a meeting that was to inaugurate a new phase in the Movement's history, and she wanted Marjorie because she particularly wanted a daring, liberal, and spiritually amorous bishop, who had once told her with a note of profound conviction that Marjorie was a very beautiful woman. She was so intent upon her purpose that she scarcely noticed Trafford. He slipped from the room unobserved under cover of her playful preliminaries, and went to the untidy little apartment overhead which served in that house as his study. He sat down at the big desk, pushed his methodically arranged papers back, and drummed on the edge with his fingers.

"I'm damned if we have that bigger house," said Trafford.

§ 6

He felt he wanted to confirm and establish this new resolution, to go right away to Labrador for a year. He wanted to tell someone the thing definitely. He would have gone downstairs again to Marjorie, but she was submerged and swimming desperately against the voluble rapids of Aunt Plessington's purpose. It might be an hour before that attack withdrew. Presently there would be other callers. He decided to have tea with his mother and talk to her about this new break in the course of his life.

Except that her hair was now grey and her brown eyes by so much contrast brighter, Mrs. Trafford's appearance had altered very little in the ten years of her only son's marriage. Whatever fresh realizations of the inevitably widening separation between parent and child these years had brought her, she had kept to herself. She had watched her daughter-in-law sometimes with sympathy, sometimes with perplexity, always with a jealous resolve to let no shadow of jealousy fall between them. Marjorie had been sweet and friendly to her, but after the first outburst of enthusiastic affection, she had neither offered nor invited confidences. Old Mrs. Trafford had talked of Marjorie to her son guardedly, and had marked and respected a growing indisposition on his part to discuss his wife. For a year or so after his marriage she had ached at times with a sense of nearly intolerable loneliness, and then the new interests she had found for herself had won their way against this depression. The new insurrectionary movement of women that had distinguished those years had attacked her by its emotion and repelled her by its crudity, and she had resolved, quite in the spirit of the man who had shaped her life, to make a systematic study of all the contributory strands that met in this difficult tangle. She tried to write, but she found that the poetic gift, the gift of the creative and illuminating phrase which alone justifies writing, was denied to her, and so she sought to make herself wise, to read and hear, and discuss and think over these things, and perhaps at last inspire and encourage writing in others.

Her circle of intimates grew, and she presently remarked with a curious interest that while she had lost the confidences of her own son and his wife, she was becoming the confidant of an increasing number of other people. They came to her, she perceived, because she was receptive and sympathetic and without a claim upon them or any interest to complicate the freedoms of their speech with her. They came to her, because she did not belong to them nor they to her. It is, indeed, the defect of all formal and established relationship, that it embarrasses speech, and taints each phase in intercourse with the flavour of diplomacy. One can be far more easily outspoken to a casual stranger one may never see again than to that inseparable other, who may misinterpret, who may disapprove or misunderstand, and who will certainly in the measure of that discord remember....

It became at last a matter of rejoicing to Mrs. Trafford that the ties of the old instinctive tenderness between herself and her son, the memories of pain and tears and the passionate conflict of childhood, were growing so thin and lax and inconsiderable, that she could even hope some day to talk to him again—almost as she talked to the young men and young women who drifted out of the unknown to her and sat in her little room and sought to express their perplexities and listened to her advice....

It seemed to her that afternoon the wished-for day had come.

Trafford found her just returned from a walk in Kensington Gardens and writing a note at her desk under the narrow sunlit window that looked upon the High Street. "Finish your letter, little mother," he said, and took possession of the hearthrug.

When she had sealed and addressed her letter, she turned her head and found him looking at his father's portrait.

"Done?" he asked, becoming aware of her eyes.

She took her letter into the hall and returned to him, closing the door behind her.

"I'm going away, little mother," he said with an unconvincing off-handedness. "I'm going to take a holiday."

"Alone?"

"Yes. I want a change. I'm going off somewhere—untrodden ground as near as one can get it nowadays—Labrador."

Their eyes met for a moment.

"Is it for long?"

"The best part of a year."

"I thought you were going on with your research work again."

"No." He paused. "I'm going to Labrador."

"Why?" she asked.

"I'm going to think."

She found nothing to say for a moment. "It's good," she remarked, "to think." Then, lest she herself should seem to be thinking too enormously, she rang the bell to order the tea that was already on its way.

"It surprises a mother," she said, when the maid had come and gone, "when her son surprises her."

"You see," he repeated, as though it explained everything, "I want to think."

Then after a pause she asked some questions about Labrador; wasn't it very cold, very desert, very dangerous and bitter, and he answered informingly. How was he going to stay there? He would go up the country with an expedition, build a hut and remain behind. Alone? Yes—thinking. Her eyes rested on his face for a time. "It will be— lonely," she said after a pause.

She saw him as a little still speck against immense backgrounds of snowy wilderness.

The tea-things came before mother and son were back at essentials again. Then she asked abruptly: "Why are you going away like this?"

"I'm tired of all this business and finance," he said after a pause.

"I thought you would be," she answered as deliberately.

"Yes. I've had enough of things. I want to get clear. And begin again somehow."

She felt they both hung away from the essential aspect. Either he or she must approach it. She decided that she would, that it was a less difficult thing for her than for him.

"And Marjorie?" she asked.

He looked into his mother's eyes very quietly. "You see," he went on deliberately disregarding her question, "I'm beached. I'm aground. I'm spoilt now for the old researches—spoilt altogether. And I don't like this life I'm leading. I detest it. While I was struggling it had a kind of interest. There was an excitement in piling up the first twenty thousand. But now—! It's empty, it's aimless, it's incessant...."

He paused. She turned to the tea-things, and lit the spirit lamp under the kettle. It seemed a little difficult to do, and her hand trembled. When she turned on him again it was with an effort.

"Does Marjorie like the life you are leading?" she asked, and pressed her lips together tightly.

He spoke with a bitterness in his voice that astonished her. "Oh, she likes it."

"Are you sure?"

He nodded.

"She won't like it without you."

"Oh, that's too much! It's her world. It's what she's done—what she's made. She can have it; she can keep it. I've played my part and got it for her. But now—now I'm free to go. I will go. She's got everything else. I've done my half of the bargain. But my soul's my own. If I want to go away and think, I will. Not even Marjorie shall stand in the way of that."

She made no answer to this outburst for a couple of seconds. Then she threw out,

"Why shouldn't Marjorie think, too?"

He considered that for some moments. "She doesn't," he said, as though the words came from the roots of his being.

"But you two——"

"We don't talk. It's astonishing—how we don't. We don't. We can't. We try to, and we can't. And she goes her way, and now—I will go mine."

"And leave her?"

He nodded.

"In London?"

"With all the things she cares for."

"Except yourself."

"I'm only a means——"

She turned her quiet face to him. "You know," she said, "that isn't true."...

"No," she repeated, to his silent contradiction.

"I've watched her," she went on. "You're not a means. I'd have spoken long ago if I had thought that. Haven't I watched? Haven't I lain awake through long nights thinking about her and you, thinking over every casual mood, every little sign—longing to help—helpless." ... She struggled with herself, for she was weeping. "It has come to this," she said in a whisper, and choked back a flood of tears.

Trafford stood motionless, watching her. She became active. She moved round the table. She looked at the kettle, moved the cups needlessly, made tea, and stood waiting for a moment before she poured it out. "It's so hard to talk to you," she said, "and about all this.... I care so much. For her. And for you.... Words don't come, dear.... One says stupid things."

She poured out the tea, and left the cups steaming, and came and stood before him.

"You see," she said, "you're ill. You aren't just. You've come to an end. You don't know where you are and what you want to do. Neither does she, my dear. She's as aimless as you—and less able to help it. Ever so much less able."

"But she doesn't show it. She goes on. She wants things and wants things——"

"And you want to go away. It's the same thing. It's exactly the same thing. It's dissatisfaction. Life leaves you empty and craving—leaves you with nothing to do but little immediate things that turn to dust as you do them. It's her trouble, just as it's your trouble."

"But she doesn't show it."

"Women don't. Not so much. Perhaps even she doesn't know it. Half the women in our world don't know—and for a woman it's so much easier to go on—so many little things."...

Trafford tried to grasp the intention of this. "Mother," he said, "I mean to go away."

"But think of her!"

"I've thought. Now I've got to think of myself."

"You can't—without her."

"I will. It's what I'm resolved to do."

"Go right away?"

"Right away."

"And think?"

He nodded.

"Find out—what it all means, my boy?"

"Yes. So far as I'm concerned."

"And then——?"

"Come back, I suppose. I haven't thought."

"To her?"

He didn't answer. She went and stood beside him, leaning upon the mantel. "Godwin," she said, "she'd only be further behind.... You've got to take her with you."

He stood still and silent.

"You've got to think things out with her. If you don't——"

"I can't."

"Then you ought to go away with her——" She stopped.

"For good?" he asked.

"Yes."

They were both silent for a space. Then Mrs. Trafford gave her mind to the tea that was cooling in the cups, and added milk and sugar. She spoke again with the table between them.

"I've thought so much of these things," she said with the milk-jug in her hand. "It's not only you two, but others. And all the movement about us.... Marriage isn't what it was. It's become a different thing because women have become human beings. Only—— You know, Godwin, all these things are so difficult to express. Woman's come out of being a slave, and yet she isn't an equal.... We've had a sort of sham emancipation, and we haven't yet come to the real one."

She put down the milk-jug on the tray with an air of grave deliberation. "If you go away from her and make the most wonderful discoveries about life and yourself, it's no good—unless she makes them too. It's no good at all.... You can't live without her in the end, any more than she can live without you. You may think you can, but I've watched you. You don't want to go away from her, you want to go away from the world that's got hold of her, from the dresses and parties and the competition and all this complicated flatness we have to live in.... It wouldn't worry you a bit, if it hadn't got hold of her. You don't want to get out of it for your own sake. You are out of it. You are as much out of it as any one can be. Only she holds you in it, because she isn't out of it. Your going away will do nothing. She'll still be in it—and still have her hold on you.... You've got to take her away. Or else—if you go away—in the end it will be just like a ship, Godwin, coming back to its moorings."

She watched his thoughtful face for some moments, then arrested herself just in time in the act of putting a second portion of sugar into each of the cups. She handed her son his tea, and he took it mechanically. "You're a wise little mother," he said. "I didn't see things in that light.... I wonder if you're right."

"I know I am," she said.

"I've thought more and more,—it was Marjorie."

"It's the world."

"Women made the world. All the dress and display and competition."

Mrs. Trafford thought. "Sex made the world. Neither men nor women. But the world has got hold of the women tighter than it has the men. They're deeper in." She looked up into his face. "Take her with you," she said, simply.

"She won't come," said Trafford, after considering it.

Mrs. Trafford reflected. "She'll come—if you make her," she said.

"She'll want to bring two housemaids."

"I don't think you know Marjorie as well as I do."

"But she can't——"

"She can. It's you—you'll want to take two housemaids for her. Even you.... Men are not fair to women."

Trafford put his untasted tea upon the mantelshelf, and confronted his mother with a question point blank. "Does Marjorie care for me?" he asked.

"You're the sun of her world."

"But she goes her way."

"She's clever, she's full of life, full of activities, eager to make and arrange and order; but there's nothing she is, nothing she makes, that doesn't centre on you."

"But if she cared, she'd understand!"

"My dear, do you understand?"

He stood musing. "I had everything clear," he said. "I saw my way to Labrador...."

Her little clock pinged the hour. "Good God!" he said, "I'm to be at dinner somewhere at seven. We're going to a first night. With the Bernards, I think. Then I suppose we'll have a supper. Always life is being slashed to tatters by these things. Always. One thinks in snatches of fifty minutes. It's dementia...."

§ 7

They dined at the Loretto Restaurant with the Bernards and Richard Hampden and Mrs. Godwin Capes, the dark-eyed, quiet-mannered wife of the dramatist, a woman of impulsive speech and long silences, who had subsided from an early romance (Capes had been divorced for her while she was still a mere girl) into a markedly correct and exclusive mother of daughters. Through the dinner Marjorie was watching Trafford and noting the deep preoccupation of his manner. He talked a little to Mrs. Bernard until it was time for Hampden to entertain her, then finding Mrs. Capes was interested in Bernard, he lapsed into thought. Presently Marjorie discovered his eyes scrutinizing herself.

She hoped the play would catch his mind, but the play seemed devised to intensify his sense of the tawdry unreality of contemporary life. Bernard filled the intervals with a conventional enthusiasm. Capes didn't appear.

"He doesn't seem to care to see his things," his wife explained.

"It's so brilliant," said Bernard.

"He has to do it," said Mrs. Capes slowly, her sombre eyes estimating the crowded stalls below. "It isn't what he cares to do."

The play was in fact an admirable piece of English stagecraft, and it dealt exclusively with that unreal other world of beings the English theatre has for its own purposes developed. Just as Greece through the ages evolved and polished and perfected the idealized life of its Homeric poems, so the British mind has evolved their Stage Land to embody its more honourable dreams, full of heroic virtues, incredible honour, genial worldliness, childish villainies, profound but amiable waiters and domestics, pathetic shepherds and preposterous crimes. Capes, needing an income, had mastered the habits and customs of this imagined world as one learns a language; success endorsed his mastery; he knew exactly how deeply to underline an irony and just when it is fit and proper for a good man to call upon "God!" or cry out "Damn!" In this play he had invented a situation in which a charming and sympathetic lady had killed a gross and drunken husband in self-defence, almost but not quite accidentally, and had then appealed to the prodigious hero for assistance in the resulting complications. At a great cost of mental suffering to himself he had told his First and Only Lie to shield her. Then years after he had returned to England—the first act happened, of course in India—to find her on the eve of marrying, without any of the preliminary confidences common among human beings, an old school friend of his. (In plays all Gentlemen have been at school together, and one has been the other's fag.) The audience had to be interested in the problem of what the prodigious hero was to do in this prodigious situation. Should he maintain a colossal silence, continue his shielding, and let his friend marry the murderess saved by his perjury, or——?... The dreadful quandary! Indeed, the absolute—inconvenience!

Marjorie watched Trafford in the corner of the box, as he listened rather contemptuously to the statement of the evening's Problem and then lapsed again into a brooding quiet. She wished she understood his moods better. She felt there was more in this than a mere resentment at her persistence about the new house....

Why didn't he go on with things?...

This darkling mood of his had only become manifest to her during the last three or four years of their life. Previously, of course, he had been irritable at times.

Were they less happy now than they had been in the little house in Chelsea? It had really been a horrible little house. And yet there had been a brightness then—a nearness....

She found her mind wandering away upon a sort of stock-taking expedition. How much of real happiness had she and Trafford had together? They ought by every standard to be so happy....

She declined the Bernard's invitation to a chafing-dish supper, and began to talk so soon as she and Trafford had settled into the car.

"Rag," she said, "something's the matter?"

"Well—yes."

"The house?"

"Yes—the house."

Marjorie considered through a little interval.

"Old man, why are you so prejudiced against a bigger house?"

"Oh, because the one we have bores me, and the next one will bore me more."

"But try it."

"I don't want to."

"Well," she said and lapsed into silence.

"And then," he asked, "what are we going to do?"

"Going to do—when?"

"After the new house——"

"I'm going to open out," she said.

He made no answer.

"I want to open out. I want you to take your place in the world, the place you deserve."

"A four-footman place?"

"Oh! the house is only a means."

He thought upon that. "A means," he asked, "to what? Look here, Marjorie, what do you think you are up to with me and yourself? What do you see me doing—in the years ahead?"

She gave him a silent and thoughtful profile for a second or so.

"At first I suppose you are going on with your researches."

"Well?"

"Then——I must tell you what I think of you, Rag. Politics——"

"Good Lord!"

"You've a sort of power. You could make things noble."

"And then? Office?"

"Why not? Look at the little men they are."

"And then perhaps a still bigger house?"

"You're not fair to me."

He pulled up the bearskin over his knees.

"Marjorie!" he said. "You see——We aren't going to do any of those things at all....
No!..."

"I can't go on with my researches," he explained. "That's what you don't understand.
I'm not able to get back to work. I shall never do any good research again. That's the
real trouble, Marjorie, and it makes all the difference. As for politics——I can't touch
politics. I despise politics. I think this empire and the monarchy and Lords and
Commons and patriotism and social reform and all the rest of it, silly, silly beyond
words; temporary, accidental, foolish, a mere stop-gap—like a gipsey's roundabout in
a place where one will presently build a house.... You don't help make the house by
riding on the roundabout.... There's no clear knowledge—no clear purpose.... Only
research matters—and expression perhaps—I suppose expression is a sort of
research—until we get that—that sufficient knowledge. And you see, I can't take up
my work again. I've lost something...."

She waited.

"I've got into this stupid struggle for winning money," he went on, "and I feel like a woman must feel who's made a success of prostitution. I've been prostituted. I feel like some one fallen and diseased.... Business and prostitution; they're the same thing. All business is a sort of prostitution, all prostitution is a sort of business. Why should one sell one's brains any more than one sells one's body?... It's so easy to succeed if one has good brains and cares to do it, and doesn't let one's attention or imagination wander—and it's so degrading. Hopelessly degrading.... I'm sick of this life, Marjorie. I don't want to buy things. I'm sick of buying. I'm at an end. I'm clean at an end. It's exactly as though suddenly in walking through a great house one came on a passage that ended abruptly in a door, which opened—on nothing! Nothing!"

"This is a mood," she whispered to his pause.

"It isn't a mood, it's a fact.... I've got nothing ahead, and I don't know how to get back. My life's no good to me any more. I've spent myself."

She looked at him with dismayed eyes. "But," she said, "this is a mood."

"No," he said, "no mood, but conviction. I know...."

He started. The car had stopped at their house, and Malcolm was opening the door of the car. They descended silently, and went upstairs in silence.

He came into her room presently and sat down by her fireside. She had gone to her dressing-table and unfastened a necklace; now with this winking and glittering in her hand she came and stood beside him.

"Rag," she said, "I don't know what to say. This isn't so much of a surprise.... I felt that somehow life was disappointing you, that I was disappointing you. I've felt it endless times, but more so lately. I haven't perhaps dared to let myself know just how much.... But isn't it what life is? Doesn't every wife disappoint her husband? We're none of us inexhaustible. After all, we've had a good time; isn't it a little ungrateful to forget?..."

"Look here, Rag," she said. "I don't know what to do. If I did know, I would do it.... What are we to do?"

"Think," he suggested.

"We've got to live as well as think."

"It's the immense troublesome futility of—everything," he said.

"Well—let us cease to be futile. Let us do. You say there is no grip for you in research, that you despise politics.... There's no end of trouble and suffering. Cannot we do social work, social reform, change the lives of others less fortunate than ourselves...."

"Who are we that we should tamper with the lives of others?"

"But one must do something."

He thought that over.

"No," he said "that's the universal blunder nowadays. One must do the right thing. And we don't know the right thing, Marjorie. That's the very heart of the trouble.... Does this life satisfy you? If it did would you always be so restless?..."

"But," she said, "think of the good things in life?"

"It's just the good, the exquisite things in life, that make me rebel against this life we are leading. It's because I've seen the streaks of gold that I know the rest for dirt. When I go cheating and scheming to my office, and come back to find you squandering yourself upon a horde of chattering, overdressed women, when I think that that is our substance and everyday and what we are, then it is I remember most the deep and beautiful things.... It is impossible, dear, it is intolerable that life was made beautiful for us—just for these vulgarities."

"Isn't there——" She hesitated. "Love—still?"

"But——Has it been love? Love is a thing that grows. But we took it—as people take flowers out of a garden, cut them off, put them in water.... How much of our daily life has been love? How much of it mere consequences of the love we've left behind us?... We've just cohabited and 'made love'—you and I—and thought of a thousand other things...."

He looked up at her. "Oh, I love a thousand things about you," he said. "But do I love you, Marjorie? Have I got you? Haven't I lost you—haven't we both lost something, the very heart of it all? Do you think that we were just cheated by instinct, that there wasn't something in it we felt and thought was there? And where is it now? Where is that brightness and wonder, Marjorie, and the pride and the immense unlimited hope?"

She was still for a moment, then knelt very swiftly before him and held out her arms.

"Oh Rag!" she said, with a face of tender beauty.

He took her finger tips in his, dropped them and stood up above her.

"My dear," he cried, "my dear! why do you always want to turn love into—touches?... Stand up again. Stand up there, my dear; don't think I've ceased to love you, but stand up there and let me talk to you as one man to another. If we let this occasion slide to embraces...."

He stopped short.

She crouched before the fire at his feet. "Go on," she said, "go on."

"I feel now that all our lives now, Marjorie——We have come to a crisis. I feel that now——now is the time. Either we shall save ourselves now or we shall never save ourselves. It is as if something had gathered and accumulated and could wait no longer. If we do not seize this opportunity——Then our lives will go on as they have gone on, will become more and more a matter of small excitements and elaborate comforts and distraction...."

He stopped this halting speech and then broke out again.

"Oh! why should the life of every day conquer us? Why should generation after generation of men have these fine beginnings, these splendid dreams of youth, attempt so much, achieve so much and then, then become—this! Look at this room, this litter of little satisfactions! Look at your pretty books there, a hundred minds you have pecked at, bright things of the spirit that attracted you as jewels attract a jackdaw. Look at the glass and silver, and that silk from China! And we are in the full tide of our years, Marjorie. Now is the very crown and best of our lives. And this is what we do, we sample, we accumulate. For this we loved, for this we hoped. Do you remember when we were young—that life seemed so splendid—it was intolerable we should ever die?... The splendid dream! The intimations of greatness!... The miserable failure!"

He raised clenched fists. "I won't stand it, Marjorie. I won't endure it. Somehow, in some way, I will get out of this life—and you with me. I have been brooding upon this and brooding, but now I know...."

"But how?" asked Marjorie, with her bare arms about her knees, staring into the fire. "How?"

"We must get out of its constant interruptions, its incessant vivid, petty appeals...."

"We might go away—to Switzerland."

"We went to Switzerland. Didn't we agree—it was our second honeymoon. It isn't a honeymoon we need. No, we'll have to go further than that."

A sudden light broke upon Marjorie's mind. She realized he had a plan. She lifted a fire-lit face to him and looked at him with steady eyes and asked——

"Where?"

"Ever so much further."

"Where?"

"I don't know."

"You do. You've planned something."

"I don't know, Marjorie. At least—I haven't made up my mind. Where it is very lonely. Cold and remote. Away from all this——" His mind stopped short, and he ended with a cry: "Oh! God! how I want to get out of all this!"

He sat down in her arm-chair, and bowed his face on his hands.

Then abruptly he stood up and went out of the room.

§ 8

When in five minutes' time he came back into her room she was still upon her hearthrug before the fire, with her necklace in her hand, the red reflections of the flames glowing and winking in her jewels and in her eyes. He came and sat again in her chair.

"I have been ranting," he said. "I feel I've been—eloquent. You make me feel like an actor-manager, in a play by Capes.... You are the most difficult person for me to talk to in all the world—because you mean so much to me."

She moved impulsively and checked herself and crouched away from him. "I mustn't touch your hand," she whispered.

"I want to explain."

"You've got to explain."

"I've got quite a definite plan.... But a sort of terror seized me. It was like—shyness."

"I know. I knew you had a plan."

"You see.... I mean to go to Labrador."

He leant forward with his elbows on his knees and his hands extended, explanatory. He wanted intensely that she should understand and agree and his desire made him clumsy, now slow and awkward, now glibly and unsatisfyingly eloquent. But she comprehended his quality better than he knew. They were to go away to Labrador, this snowy desert of which she had scarcely heard, to camp in the very heart of the wilderness, two hundred miles or more from any human habitation——

"But how long?" she asked abruptly.

"The better part of a year."

"And we are to talk?"

"Yes," he said, "talk and think ourselves together—oh!—the old phrases carry it all— find God...."

"It is what I dreamt of, Rag, years ago."

"Will you come," he cried, "out of all this?"

She leant across the hearthrug, and seized and kissed his hand....

Then, with one of those swift changes of hers, she was in revolt. "But, Rag," she exclaimed, "this is dreaming. We are not free. There are the children! Rag! We cannot leave the children!"

"We can," he said. "We must."

"But, my dear!—our duty!"

"Is it a mother's duty always to keep with her children? They will be looked after, their lives are organized, there is my mother close at hand.... What is the good of having children at all—unless their world is to be better than our world?... What are we doing to save them from the same bathos as this—to which we have come? We give them food and health and pictures and lessons, that's all very well while they are just little children; but we've got no religion to give them, no aim, no sense of a general purpose. What is the good of bread and health—and no worship?... What can we say to them when they ask us why we brought them into the world?—We happened—you happened. What are we to tell them when they demand the purpose of all this training, all these lessons? When they ask what we are preparing them for? Just that you, too, may have children! Is that any answer? Marjorie, it's common-sense to try this over—to make this last supreme effort—just as it will be common-sense to separate if we can't get the puzzle solved together."

"Separate!"

"Separate. Why not? We can afford it. Of course, we shall separate."

"But Rag!—separate!"

He faced her protest squarely. "Life is not worth living," he said, "unless it has more to hold it together than ours has now. If we cannot escape together, then—I will go alone."...

§ 9

They parted that night resolved to go to Labrador together, with the broad outline of their subsequent journey already drawn. Each lay awake far into the small hours thinking of this purpose and of one another, with a strange sense of renewed association. Each woke to a morning of sunshine heavy-eyed. Each found that overnight decision remote and incredible. It was like something in a book or a play that had moved them very deeply. They came down to breakfast, and helped themselves after the wonted fashion of several years, Marjorie with a skilful eye to the large order of her household; the Times had one or two characteristic letters which interested them both; there was the usual picturesque irruption of the children and a distribution of early strawberries among them. Trafford had two notes in his correspondence which threw a new light upon the reconstruction of the Norton-Batsford company in which he was interested; he formed a definite conclusion upon the situation, and went quite normally to his study and the telephone to act upon that.

It was only as the morning wore on that it became real to him that he and Marjorie had decided to leave the world. Then, with the Norton-Batsford business settled, he sat at his desk and mused. His apathy passed. His imagination began to present first one picture and then another of his retreat. He walked along Oxford Street to his Club thinking—"soon we shall be out of all this." By the time he was at lunch in his Club, Labrador had become again the magic refuge it had seemed the day before. After lunch he went to work in the library, finding out books about Labrador, and looking up the details of the journey.

But his sense of futility and hopeless oppression had vanished. He walked along the corridor and down the great staircase, and without a trace of the despairful hostility of the previous day, passed Blenkins, talking grey bosh with infinite thoughtfulness. He nodded easily to Blenkins. He was going out of it all, as a man might do who discovers after years of weary incarceration that the walls of his cell are made of thin paper. The time when Blenkins seemed part of a prison-house of routine and invincible stupidity seemed ten ages ago.

In Pall Mall Trafford remarked Lady Grampians and the Countess of Claridge, two women of great influence, in a big green car, on the way no doubt to create or sustain or destroy; and it seemed to him that it was limitless ages since these poor old dears with their ridiculous hats and their ridiculous airs, their luncheons and dinners and dirty aggressive old minds, had sent tidal waves of competitive anxiety into his home....

He found himself jostling through the shopping crowd on the sunny side of Regent Street. He felt now that he looked over the swarming, preoccupied heads at distant things. He and Marjorie were going out of it all, going clean out of it all. They were going to escape from society and shopping, and petty engagements and incessant triviality—as a bird flies up out of weeds.

But Marjorie fluctuated more than he did.

There were times when the expedition for which he was now preparing rapidly and methodically seemed to her the most adventurously-beautiful thing that had ever come to her, and times when it seemed the maddest and most hopeless of eccentricities. There were times when she had devastating premonitions of filth, hunger, strain and fatigue, damp and cold, when her whole being recoiled from the project, when she could even think of staying secure in London and letting him go alone. She developed complicated anxieties for the children; she found reasons for further inquiries, for delay. "Why not," she suggested, "wait a year?"

"No," he said, "I won't. I mean we are to do this, and do it now, and nothing but sheer physical inability to do it will prevent my carrying it out.... And you? Of course you are to come. I can't drag you shrieking all the way to Labrador; short of that I'm going to make you come with me."

She sat and looked up at him with dark lights in her upturned eyes, and a little added warmth in her cheek. "You've never forced my will like this before," she said, in a low voice. "Never."

He was too intent upon his own resolve to heed her tones.

"It hasn't seemed necessary somehow," he said, considering her statement. "Now it does."

"This is something final," she said.

"It is final."

She found an old familiar phrasing running through her head, as she sat crouched together, looking up at his rather gaunt, very intent face, the speech of another woman echoing to her across a vast space of years: "Whither thou goest I will go——"

"In Labrador," he began....

CHAPTER THE THIRD

The Pilgrimage to Lonely Hut

§ 1

Marjorie was surprised to find how easy it was at last to part from her children and go with Trafford.

"I am not sorry," she said, "not a bit sorry—but I am fearfully afraid. I shall dream they are ill.... Apart from that, it's strange how you grip me and they don't...."

In the train to Liverpool she watched Trafford with the queer feeling which comes to all husbands and wives at times that that other partner is indeed an undiscovered stranger, just beginning to show perplexing traits,—full of inconceivable possibilities.

For some reason his tearing her up by the roots in this fashion had fascinated her imagination. She felt a strange new wonder at him that had in it just a pleasant faint flavour of fear. Always before she had felt a curious aversion and contempt for those servile women who are said to seek a master, to want to be mastered, to be eager even for the physical subjugations of brute force. Now she could at least understand, sympathize even with them. Not only Trafford surprised her but herself. She found she was in an unwonted perplexing series of moods. All her feelings struck her now as being incorrect as well as unexpected; not only had life become suddenly full of novelty but she was making novel responses. She felt that she ought to be resentful and tragically sorry for her home and children. She felt this departure ought to have the quality of an immense sacrifice, a desperate and heroic undertaking for Trafford's sake. Instead she could detect little beyond an adventurous exhilaration when presently she walked the deck of the steamer that was to take her to St. John's. She had visited her cabin, seen her luggage stowed away, and now she surveyed the Mersey and its shipping with a renewed freshness of mind. She was reminded of the day, now nearly nine years ago, when she had crossed the sea for the first time—to Italy. Then, too, Trafford had seemed a being of infinitely wonderful possibilities.... What were the children doing?—that ought to have been her preoccupation. She didn't know; she didn't care! Trafford came and stood beside her, pointed out this and that upon the landing stage, no longer heavily sullen, but alert, interested, almost gay....

Neither of them could find any way to the great discussion they had set out upon, in this voyage to St. John's. But there was plenty of time before them. Plenty of time! They were both the prey of that uneasy distraction which seems the inevitable quality of a passenger steamship. They surveyed and criticized their fellow travellers, and prowled up and down through the long swaying days and the cold dark nights. They slept uneasily amidst fog-horn hootings and the startling sounds of waves swirling against the ports. Marjorie had never had a long sea voyage before; for the first time in her life she saw all the world, through a succession of days, as a circle of endless blue waters, with the stars and planets and sun and moon rising sharply from its rim. Until one has had a voyage no one really understands that old Earth is a watery globe.... They ran into thirty hours of storm, which subsided, and then came a slow time among icebergs, and a hooting, dreary passage through fog. The first three icebergs were marvels, the rest bores; a passing collier out of her course and pitching heavily, a lonely black and dirty ship with a manner almost derelict, filled their thoughts for half a day. Their minds were in a state of tedious inactivity, eager for such small interests and only capable of such small interests. There was no hurry to talk, they agreed, no hurry at all, until they were settled away ahead there among the snows. "There we shall have plenty of time for everything...."

Came the landfall and then St. John's, and they found themselves side by side watching the town draw near. The thought of landing and transference to another ship refreshed them both....

They were going, Trafford said, in search of God, but it was far more like two children starting out upon a holiday.

§ 2

There was trouble and procrastination about the half-breed guides that Trafford had arranged should meet them at St. John's, and it was three weeks from their reaching Newfoundland before they got themselves and their guides and equipment and general stores aboard the boat for Port Dupré. Thence he had planned they should go in the Gibson schooner to Manivikovik, the Marconi station at the mouth of the Green River, and thence past the new pulp-mills up river to the wilderness. There were delays and a few trivial, troublesome complications in carrying out this scheme, but at last a day came when Trafford could wave good-bye to the seven people and eleven dogs which constituted the population of Peter Hammond's, that last rude outpost of civilization twenty miles above the pulp-mill, and turn his face in good earnest towards the wilderness.

Neither he nor Marjorie looked back at the headland for a last glimpse of the little settlement they were leaving. Each stared ahead over the broad, smooth sweep of water, broken by one transverse bar of foaming shallows, and scanned the low, tree-clad hills beyond that drew together at last in the distant gorge out of which the river came. The morning was warm and full of the promise of a hot noon, so that the veils they wore against the assaults of sand-flies and mosquitoes were already a little inconvenient. It seemed incredible in this morning glow that the wooded slopes along the shore of the lake were the border of a land in which nearly half the inhabitants die of starvation. The deep-laden canoes swept almost noiselessly through the water with a rhythmic alternation of rush and pause as the dripping paddles drove and returned. Altogether there were four long canoes and five Indian breeds in their party, and when they came to pass through shallows both Marjorie and Trafford took a paddle.

They came to the throat of the gorge towards noon, and found strong flowing deep water between its high purple cliffs. All hands had to paddle again, and it was only when they came to rest in a pool to eat a mid-day meal and afterwards to land upon a mossy corner for a stretch and a smoke, that Marjorie discovered the peculiar beauty of the rock about them. On the dull purplish-grey surfaces played the most extraordinary mist of luminous iridescence. It fascinated her. Here was a land whose common substance had this gemlike opalescence. But her attention was very soon withdrawn from these glancing splendours.

She had had to put aside her veil to eat, and presently she felt the vividly painful stabs of the black-fly and discovered blood upon her face. A bigger fly, the size and something of the appearance of a small wasp, with an evil buzz, also assailed her and Trafford. It was a bad corner for flies; the breeds even were slapping their wrists and swearing under the torment, and every one was glad to embark and push on up the winding gorge. It opened out for a time, and then the wooded shores crept in again, and in another half-hour they saw ahead of them a long rush of foaming waters among tumbled rocks that poured down from a brimming, splashing line of light against the sky. They crossed the river, ran the canoes into an eddy under the shelter of a big stone and began to unload. They had reached their first portage.

The rest of the first day was spent in packing and lugging first the cargoes and then the canoes up through thickets and over boulders and across stretches of reindeer moss for the better part of two miles to a camping ground about half-way up the rapids.

Marjorie and Trafford tried to help with the carrying, but this evidently shocked and distressed the men too much, so they desisted and set to work cutting wood and gathering moss for the fires and bedding for the camp. When the iron stove was brought up the man who had carried it showed them how to put it up on stakes and start a fire in it, and then Trafford went to the river to get water, and Marjorie made a kind of flour cake in the frying-pan in the manner an American woman from the wilderness had once shown her, and boiled water for tea. The twilight had deepened to night while the men were still stumbling up the trail with the last two canoes.

It gave Marjorie a curiously homeless feeling to stand there in the open with the sunset dying away below the black scrubby outlines of the treetops uphill to the northwest, and to realize the nearest roof was already a day's toilsome journey away. The cool night breeze blew upon her bare face and arms—for now the insects had ceased from troubling and she had cast aside gloves and veil and turned up her sleeves to cook—and the air was full of the tumult of the rapids tearing seaward over the rocks below. Struggling through the bushes towards her was an immense, headless quadruped with unsteady legs and hesitating paces, two of the men carrying the last canoe. Two others were now assisting Trafford to put up the little tent that was to shelter her, and the fifth was kneeling beside her very solemnly and respectfully cutting slices of bacon for her to fry. The air was very sweet, and she wished she could sleep not in the tent but under the open sky.

It was queer, she thought, how much of the wrappings of civilization had slipped from them already. Every day of the journey from London had released them or deprived them—she hardly knew which—of a multitude of petty comforts and easy accessibilities. The afternoon toil uphill intensified the effect of having clambered up out of things—to this loneliness, this twilight openness, this simplicity.

The men ate apart at a fire they made for themselves, and after Trafford and Marjorie had supped on damper, bacon and tea, he smoked. They were both too healthily tired to talk very much. There was no moon but a frosty brilliance of stars, the air which had been hot and sultry at mid-day grew keen and penetrating, and after she had made him tell her the names of constellations she had forgotten, she suddenly perceived the wisdom of the tent, went into it—it was sweet and wonderful with sprigs of the Labrador tea-shrub—undressed, and had hardly rolled herself up into a cocoon of blankets before she was fast asleep.

She was awakened by a blaze of sunshine pouring into the tent, a smell of fried bacon and Trafford's voice telling her to get up. "They've gone on with the first loads," he said. "Get up, wrap yourself in a blanket, and come and bathe in the river. It's as cold as ice."

She blinked at him. "Aren't you stiff?" she asked.

"I was stiffer before I bathed," he said.

She took the tin he offered her. (They weren't to see china cups again for a year.) "It's woman's work getting tea," she said as she drank.

"You can't be a squaw all at once," said Trafford.

§ 3

After Marjorie had taken her dip, dried roughly behind a bush, twisted her hair into a pigtail and coiled it under her hat, she amused herself and Trafford as they clambered up through rocks and willows to the tent again by cataloguing her apparatus of bath and toilette at Sussex Square and tracing just when and how she had parted from each item on the way to this place.

"But I say!" she cried, with a sudden, sharp note of dismay, "we haven't soap! This is our last cake almost. I never thought of soap."

"Nor I," said Trafford.

He spoke again presently. "We don't turn back for soap," he said.

"We don't turn back for anything," said Marjorie. "Still—I didn't count on a soapless winter."

"I'll manage something," said Trafford, a little doubtfully. "Trust a chemist...."

That day they finished the portage and came out upon a wide lake with sloping shores and a distant view of snow-topped mountains, a lake so shallow that at times their loaded canoes scraped on the glaciated rock below and they had to alter their course. They camped in a lurid sunset; the night was warm and mosquitoes were troublesome, and towards morning came a thunderstorm and wind and rain.

The dawn broke upon a tearing race of waves and a wild drift of slanting rain sweeping across the lake before a gale. Marjorie peered out at this as one peers out under the edge of an umbrella. It was manifestly impossible to go on, and they did nothing that day but run up a canvas shelter for the men and shift the tent behind a thicket of trees out of the full force of the wind. The men squatted stoically, and smoked and yarned. Everything got coldly wet, and for the most part the Traffords sat under the tent and stared blankly at this summer day in Labrador.

"Now," said Trafford, "we ought to begin talking."

"There's nothing much to do else," said Marjorie.

"Only one can't begin," said Trafford.

He was silent for a time. "We're getting out of things," he said....

The next day began with a fine drizzle through which the sun broke suddenly about ten o'clock. They made a start at once, and got a good dozen miles up the lake before it was necessary to camp again. Both Marjorie and Trafford felt stiff and weary and uncomfortable all day, and secretly a little doubtful now of their own endurance. They camped on an island on turf amidst slippery rocks, and the next day were in a foaming difficult river again, with glittering shallows that obliged every one to get out at times to wade and push. All through the afternoon they were greatly beset by flies. And so they worked their way on through a third days' journey towards the silent inland of Labrador.

Day followed day of toilsome and often tedious travel; they fought rapids, they waited while the men stumbled up long portages under vast loads, going and returning, they camped and discussed difficulties and alternatives. The flies sustained an unrelenting persecution, until faces were scarred in spite of veils and smoke fires, until wrists and necks were swollen and the blood in a fever. As they got higher and higher towards the central plateau, the mid-day heat increased and the nights grew colder, until they would find themselves toiling, wet with perspiration, over rocks that sheltered a fringe of ice beneath their shadows. The first fatigues and lassitudes, the shrinking from cold water, the ache of muscular effort, gave place to a tougher and tougher endurance; skin seemed to have lost half its capacity for pain without losing a tithe of its discrimination, muscles attained a steely resilience; they were getting seasoned. "I don't feel philosophical," said Trafford, "but I feel well."

"We're getting out of things."

"Suppose we are getting out of our problems!..."

One day as they paddled across a mile-long pool, they saw three bears prowling in single file high up on the hillside. "Look," said the man, and pointed with his paddle at the big, soft, furry black shapes, magnified and startling in the clear air. All the canoes rippled to a stop, the men, at first still, whispered softly. One passed a gun to Trafford, who hesitated and looked at Marjorie.

The air of tranquil assurance about these three huge loafing monsters had a queer effect on Marjorie's mind. They made her feel that they were at home and that she was an intruder. She had never in her life seen any big wild animals except in a menagerie. She had developed a sort of unconscious belief that all big wild animals were in menageries nowadays, and this spectacle of beasts entirely at large startled her. There was never a bar between these creatures, she felt, and her sleeping self. They might, she thought, do any desperate thing to feeble men and women who came their way.

"Shall I take a shot?" asked Trafford.

"No," said Marjorie, pervaded by the desire for mutual toleration. "Let them be."

The big brutes disappeared in a gully, reappeared, came out against the skyline one by one and vanished.

"Too long a shot," said Trafford, handing back the gun....

Their journey lasted altogether a month. Never once did they come upon any human being save themselves, though in one place they passed the poles—for the most part overthrown—of an old Indian encampment. But this desolation was by no means lifeless. They saw great quantities of waterbirds, geese, divers, Arctic partridge and the like, they became familiar with the banshee cry of the loon. They lived very largely on geese and partridge. Then for a time about a string of lakes, the country was alive with migrating deer going south, and the men found traces of a wolf. They killed six caribou, and stayed to skin and cut them up and dry the meat to replace the bacon they had consumed, caught, fried and ate great quantities of trout, and became accustomed to the mysterious dance of the northern lights as the sunset afterglow faded.

Everywhere, except in the river gorges, the country displayed the low hummocky lines and tarn-like pools of intensely glaciated land; everywhere it was carpeted with reindeer moss growing upon peat and variegated by bushes of flowering, sweet-smelling Labrador tea. In places this was starred with little harebells and diversified by tussocks of heather and rough grass, and over the rocks trailed delicate dwarf shrubs and a very pretty and fragrant pink-flowered plant of which neither she nor Trafford knew the name. There was an astonishing amount of wild fruit, raspberries, cranberries, and a white kind of strawberry that was very delightful. The weather, after its first outbreak, remained brightly serene....

And at last it seemed fit to Trafford to halt and choose his winter quarters. He chose a place on the side of a low, razor-hacked rocky mountain ridge, about fifty feet above the river—which had now dwindled to a thirty-foot stream. His site was near a tributary rivulet that gave convenient water, in a kind of lap that sheltered between two rocky knees, each bearing thickets of willow and balsam. Not a dozen miles away from them now they reckoned was the Height of Land, the low watershed between the waters that go to the Atlantic and those that go to Hudson's Bay. Close beside the site he had chosen a shelf of rock ran out and gave a glimpse up the narrow rocky valley of the Green River's upper waters and a broad prospect of hill and tarn towards the south-east. North and north-east of them the country rose to a line of low crests, with here and there a yellowing patch of last year's snow, and across the valley were slopes covered in places by woods of stunted pine. It had an empty spaciousness of effect; the one continually living thing seemed to be the Green River, hurrying headlong, noisily, perpetually, in an eternal flight from this high desolation. Birds were rare here, and the insects that buzzed and shrilled and tormented among the rocks and willows in the gorge came but sparingly up the slopes to them.

"Here presently," said Trafford, "we shall be in peace."

"It is very lonely," said Marjorie.

"The nearer to God."

"Think! Not one of these hills has ever had a name."

"Well?"

"It might be in some other planet."

"Oh!—we'll christen them. That shall be Marjorie Ridge, and that Rag Valley. This space shall be—oh! Bayswater! Before we've done with it, this place and every feature of it will be as familiar as Sussex Square. More so,—for half the houses there would be stranger to us, if we could see inside them, than anything in this wilderness.... As familiar, say—as your drawing-room. That's better."

Marjorie made no answer, but her eyes went from the reindeer moss and scrub and thickets of the foreground to the low rocky ridges that bounded the view north and east of them. The scattered boulders, the tangles of wood, the barren upper slopes, the dust-soiled survivals of the winter's snowfall, all contributed to an effect at once carelessly desert and hopelessly untidy. She looked westward, and her memory was full of interminable streaming rapids, wastes of ice-striated rocks, tiresome struggles through woods and wild, wide stretches of tundra and tarn, trackless and treeless, infinitely desolate. It seemed to her that the sea coast was but a step from London and ten thousand miles away from her.

§ 4

The men had engaged to build the framework of hut and store shed before returning, and to this under Trafford's direction they now set themselves. They were all half-breeds, mingling with Indian with Scottish or French blood, sober and experienced men. Three were named Mackenzie, two brothers and a cousin, and another, Raymond Noyes, was a relation and acquaintance of that George Elson who was with Wallace and Leonidas Hubbard, and afterwards guided Mrs. Hubbard in her crossing of Labrador. The fifth was a boy of eighteen named Lean. They were all familiar with the idea of summer travel in this country; quite a number, a score or so that is to say, of adventurous people, including three or four women, had ventured far in the wake of the Hubbards into these great wildernesses during the decade that followed that first tragic experiment in which Hubbard died. But that any one not of Indian or Esquimaux blood should propose to face out the Labrador winter was a new thing to them. They were really very sceptical at the outset whether these two highly civilized-looking people would ever get up to the Height of Land at all, and it was still with manifest incredulity that they set about the building of the hut and the construction of the sleeping bunks for which they had brought up planking. A stream of speculative talk had flowed along beside Marjorie and Trafford ever since they had entered the Green River; and it didn't so much come to an end as get cut off at last by the necessity of their departure.

Noyes would stand, holding a hammer and staring at the narrow little berth he was fixing together.

"You'll not sleep in this," he said.

"I will," replied Marjorie.

"You'll come back with us."

"Not me."

"There'll be wolves come and howl."

"Let 'em."

"They'll come right up to the door here. Winter makes 'em hidjus bold."

Marjorie shrugged her shoulders.

"It's that cold I've known a man have his nose froze while he lay in bed," said Noyes.

"Up here?"

"Down the coast. But they say it's 'most as cold up here. Many's the man it's starved and froze."...

He and his companions told stories,—very circumstantial and pitiful stories, of Indian disasters. They were all tales of weariness and starvation, of the cessation of food, because the fishing gave out, because the caribou did not migrate by the customary route, because the man of a family group broke his wrist, and then of the start of all or some of the party to the coast to get help and provisions, of the straining, starving fugitives caught by blizzards, losing the track, devouring small vermin raw, gnawing their own skin garments until they toiled half-naked in the snow,—becoming cannibals, becoming delirious, lying down to die. Once there was an epidemic of influenza, and three families of seven and twenty people just gave up and starved and died in their lodges, and were found, still partly frozen, a patient, pitiful company, by trappers in the spring....

Such they said, were the common things that happened in a Labrador winter. Did the Traffords wish to run such risks?

A sort of propagandist enthusiasm grew up in the men. They felt it incumbent upon them to persuade the Traffords to return. They reasoned with them rather as one does with wilful children. They tried to remind them of the delights and securities of the world they were deserting. Noyes drew fancy pictures of the pleasures of London by way of contrast to the bitter days before them. "You've got everything there, everything. Suppose you feel a bit ill, you go out, and every block there's a drug store got everything—all the new rem'dies—p'raps twenty, thirty sorts of rem'dy. Lit up, nice. And chaps in collars—like gentlemen. Or you feel a bit dully and you go into the streets and there's people. Why! when I was in New York I used to spend hours looking at the people. Hours! And everything lit up, too. Sky signs! Readin' everywhere. You can spend hours and hours in New York——"

"London," said Marjorie.

"Well, London—just going about and reading the things they stick up. Every blamed sort of thing. Or you say, let's go somewhere. Let's go out and be a bit lively. See? Up you get on a car and there you are! Great big restaurants, blazing with lights, and you can't think of a thing to eat they haven't got. Waiters all round you, dressed tremendous, fair asking you to have more. Or you say, let's go to a theatre. Very likely," said Noyes, letting his imagination soar, "you order up one of these automobillies."

"By telephone," helped Trafford.

"By telephone," confirmed Noyes. "When I was in New York there was a telephone in each room in the hotel. Each room. I didn't use it ever, except once when they didn't answer—but there it was. I know about telephones all right...."

Why had they come here? None of the men were clear about that. Marjorie and Trafford would overhear them discussing this question at their fire night after night; they seemed to talk of nothing else. They indulged in the boldest hypotheses, even in the theory that Trafford knew of deposits of diamonds and gold, and would trust no one but his wife with the secret. They seemed also attracted by the idea that our two young people had "done something."

Lean, with memories of some tattered sixpenny novel that had drifted into his hands from England, had even some notion of an elopement, of a pursuing husband or a vindictive wife. He was young and romantic, but it seemed incredible he should suggest that Marjorie was a royal princess. Yet there were moments when his manner betrayed a more than personal respect....

One night after a hard day's portage Mackenzie was inspired by a brilliant idea. "They got no children," he said, in a hoarse, exceptionally audible whisper. "It worries them. Them as is Catholics goes pilgrimages, but these ain't Catholics. See?"

"I can't stand that," said Marjorie. "It touches my pride. I've stood a good deal. Mr. Mackenzie!... Mr.... Mackenzie."

The voice at the men's fire stopped and a black head turned around. "What is it, Mrs. Trafford?" asked Mackenzie.

She held up four fingers. "Four!" she said.

"Eh?"

"Three sons and a daughter," said Marjorie.

Mackenzie did not take it in until his younger brother had repeated her words.

"And you've come from them to this.... Sir, what have you come for?"

"We want to be here," shouted Trafford to their listening pause. Their silence was incredulous.

"We wanted to be alone together. There was too much—over there—too much everything."

Mackenzie, in silhouette against the fire, shook his head, entirely dissatisfied. He could not understand how there could be too much of anything. It was beyond a trapper's philosophy.

"Come back with us sir," said Noyes. "You'll weary of it...."

Noyes clung to the idea of dissuasion to the end. "I don't care to leave ye," he said, and made a sort of byword of it that served when there was nothing else to say.

He made it almost his last words. He turned back for another handclasp as the others under their light returning packs were filing down the hill.

"I don't care to leave ye," he said.

"Good luck!" said Trafford.

"You'll need it," said Noyes, and looked at Marjorie very gravely and intently before he turned about and marched off after his fellows....

Both Marjorie and Trafford felt a queer emotion, a sense of loss and desertion, a swelling in the throat, as that file of men receded over the rocky slopes, went down into a dip, reappeared presently small and remote cresting another spur, going on towards the little wood that hid the head of the rapids. They halted for a moment on the edge of the wood and looked back, then turned again one by one and melted stride by stride into the trees. Noyes was the last to go. He stood, in an attitude that spoke as plainly as words, "I don't care to leave ye." Something white waved and flickered; he had whipped out the letters they had given him for England, and he was waving them. Then, as if by an effort, he set himself to follow the others, and the two still watchers on the height above saw him no more.

Lonely Hut

§ 1

Marjorie and Trafford walked slowly back to the hut. "There is much to do before the weather breaks," he said, ending a thoughtful silence. "Then we can sit inside there and talk about the things we need to talk about."

He added awkwardly: "Since we started, there has been so much to hold the attention. I remember a mood—an immense despair. I feel it's still somewhere at the back of things, waiting to be dealt with. It's our essential fact. But meanwhile we've been busy, looking at fresh things."

He paused. "Now it will be different perhaps...."

For nearly four weeks indeed they were occupied very closely, and crept into their bunks at night as tired as wholesome animals who drop to sleep. At any time the weather might break; already there had been two overcast days and a frowning conference of clouds in the north. When at last storms began they knew there would be nothing for it but to keep in the hut until the world froze up.

There was much to do to the hut. The absence of anything but stunted and impoverished timber and the limitation of time, had forbidden a log hut, and their home was really only a double framework, rammed tight between inner and outer frame with a mixture of earth and boughs and twigs of willow, pine and balsam. The floor was hammered earth carpeted with balsam twigs and a caribou skin. Outside and within wall and roof were faced with coarse canvas—that was Trafford's idea—and their bunks occupied two sides of the hut. Heating was done by the sheet-iron stove they had brought with them, and the smoke was carried out to the roof by a thin sheet-iron pipe which had come up outside a roll of canvas. They had made the roof with about the pitch of a Swiss châlet, and it was covered with nailed waterproof canvas, held down by a large number of big lumps of stone. Much of the canvassing still remained to do when the men went down, and then the Traffords used every scrap of packing-paper and newspaper that had come up with them and was not needed for lining the bunks in covering any crack or join in the canvas wall.

Two decadent luxuries, a rubber bath and two rubber hot-water bottles, hung behind the door. They were almost the only luxuries. Kettles and pans and some provisions stood on a shelf over the stove; there was also a sort of recess cupboard in the opposite corner, reserve clothes were in canvas trunks under the bunks, they kept their immediate supply of wood under the eaves just outside the door, and there was a big can of water between stove and door. When the winter came they would have to bring in ice from the stream.

This was their home. The tent that had sheltered Marjorie on the way up was erected close to this hut to serve as a rude scullery and outhouse, and they also made a long, roughly thatched roof with a canvas cover, supported on stakes, to shelter the rest of the stores. The stuff in tins and cases and jars they left on the ground under this; the rest—the flour, candles, bacon, dried caribou beef, and so forth, they hung, as they hoped, out of the reach of any prowling beast. And finally and most important was the wood pile. This they accumulated to the north and east of the hut, and all day long with a sort of ant-like perseverance Trafford added to it from the thickets below. Once or twice, however, tempted by the appearance of birds, he went shooting, and one day he got five geese that they spent a day upon, plucking, cleaning, boiling and putting up in all their store of empty cans, letting the fat float and solidify on the top to preserve this addition to their provision until the advent of the frost rendered all other preservatives unnecessary. They also tried to catch trout down in the river below, but though they saw many fish the catch was less than a dozen.

It was a discovery to both of them to find how companionable these occupations were, how much more side by side they could be amateurishly cleaning out a goose and disputing about its cooking, than they had ever contrived to be in Sussex Square.

"These things are so infernally interesting," said Trafford, surveying the row of miscellaneous cans upon the stove he had packed with disarticulated goose. "But we didn't come here to picnic. All this is eating us up. I have a memory of some immense tragic purpose——"

"That tin's boiling!" screamed Marjorie sharply.

He resumed his thread after an active interlude.

"We'll keep the wolf from the door," he said.

"Don't talk of wolves!" said Marjorie.

"It is only when men have driven away the wolf from the door—oh! altogether away, that they find despair in the sky? I wonder——"

"What?" asked Marjorie in his pause.

"I wonder if there is nothing really in life but this, the food hunt and the love hunt. Is life just all hunger and need, and are we left with nothing—nothing at all—when these things are done?... We're infernally uncomfortable here."

"Oh, nonsense!" cried Marjorie.

"Think of your carpets at home! Think of the great, warm, beautiful house that wasn't big enough!—And yet here, we're happy."

"We are happy," said Marjorie, struck by the thought. "Only——"

"Yes."

"I'm afraid. And I long for the children. And the wind nips."

"It may be those are good things for us. No! This is just a lark as yet, Marjorie. It's still fresh and full of distractions. The discomforts are amusing. Presently we'll get used to it. Then we'll talk out—what we have to talk out.... I say, wouldn't it keep and improve this goose of ours if we put in a little brandy?"

§ 2

The weather broke at last. One might say it smashed itself over their heads. There came an afternoon darkness swift and sudden, a wild gale and an icy sleet that gave place in the night to snow, so that Trafford looked out next morning to see a maddening chaos of small white flakes, incredibly swift, against something that was neither darkness nor light. Even with the door but partly ajar a cruelty of cold put its claw within, set everything that was moveable swaying and clattering, and made Marjorie hasten shuddering to heap fresh logs upon the fire. Once or twice Trafford went out to inspect tent and roof and store-shed, several times wrapped to the nose he battled his way for fresh wood, and for the rest of the blizzard they kept to the hut. It was slumberously stuffy, but comfortingly full of flavours of tobacco and food. There were two days of intermission and a day of gusts and icy sleet again, turning with one extraordinary clap of thunder to a wild downpour of dancing lumps of ice, and then a night when it seemed all Labrador, earth and sky together, was in hysterical protest against inconceivable wrongs.

And then the break was over; the annual freezing-up was accomplished, winter had established itself, the snowfall moderated and ceased, and an ice-bound world shone white and sunlit under a cloudless sky.

§ 3

Through all that time they got no further with the great discussion for which they had faced that solitude. They attempted beginnings.

"Where had we got to when we left England?" cried Marjorie. "You couldn't work, you couldn't rest—you hated our life."

"Yes, I know. I had a violent hatred of the lives we were leading. I thought—we had to get away. To think.... But things don't leave us alone here."

He covered his face with his hands.

"Why did we come here?" he asked.

"You wanted—to get out of things."

"Yes. But with you.... Have we, after all, got out of things at all? I said coming up, perhaps we were leaving our own problem behind. In exchange for other problems—old problems men have had before. We've got nearer necessity; that's all. Things press on us just as much. There's nothing more fundamental in wild nature, nothing profounder—only something earlier. One doesn't get out of life by going here or there.... But I wanted to get you away—from all things that had such a hold on you....

"When one lies awake at nights, then one seems to get down into things...."

He went to the door, opened it, and stood looking out. Against a wan daylight the snow was falling noiselessly and steadily.

"Everything goes on," he said.... "Relentlessly...."

§ 4

That was as far as they had got when the storms ceased and they came out again into an air inexpressibly fresh and sharp and sweet, and into a world blindingly clean and golden white under the rays of the morning sun.

"We will build a fire out here," said Marjorie; "make a great pile. There is no reason at all why we shouldn't live outside all through the day in such weather as this."

§ 5

One morning Trafford found the footmarks of some catlike creature in the snow near the bushes where he was accustomed to get firewood; they led away very plainly up the hill, and after breakfast he took his knife and rifle and snowshoes and went after the lynx—for that he decided the animal must be. There was no urgent reason why he should want to kill a lynx, unless perhaps that killing it made the store shed a trifle safer; but it was the first trail of any living thing for many days; it promised excitement; some primordial instinct perhaps urged him.

The morning was a little overcast, and very cold between the gleams of wintry sunshine. "Good-bye, dear wife!" he said, and then as she remembered afterwards came back a dozen yards to kiss her.

"I'll not be long," he said. "The beast's prowling, and if it doesn't get wind of me I ought to find it in an hour." He hesitated for a moment. "I'll not be long," he repeated, and she had an instant's wonder whether he hid from her the same dread of loneliness that she concealed. Or perhaps he only knew her secret. Up among the tumbled rocks he turned, and she was still watching him. "Good-bye!" he cried and waved, and the willow thickets closed about him.

She forced herself to the petty duties of the day, made up the fire from the pile he had left for her, set water to boil, put the hut in order, brought out sheets and blankets to air and set herself to wash up. She wished she had been able to go with him. The sky cleared presently, and the low December sun lit all the world about her, but it left her spirit desolate.

She did not expect him to return until mid-day, and she sat herself down on a log before the fire to darn a pair of socks as well as she could. For a time this unusual occupation held her attention and then her hands became slow and at last inactive, and she fell into reverie. She thought at first of her children and what they might be doing, in England across there to the east it would be about five hours later, four o'clock in the afternoon, and the children would be coming home through the warm muggy London sunshine with Fraulein Otto to tea. She wondered if they had the proper clothes, if they were well; were they perhaps quarrelling or being naughty or skylarking gaily across the Park. Of course Fraulein Otto was all right, quite to be trusted, absolutely trustworthy, and their grandmother would watch for a flushed face or an irrational petulance or any of the little signs that herald trouble with more than a mother's instinctive alertness. No need to worry about the children, no need whatever.... The world of London opened out behind these thoughts; it was so queer to think that she was in almost the same latitude as the busy bright traffic of the autumn season in Kensington Gore; that away there in ten thousand cleverly furnished drawing-rooms the ringing tea things were being set out for the rustling advent of smart callers and the quick leaping gossip. And there would be all sorts of cakes and little things; for a while her mind ran on cakes and little things, and she thought in particular whether it wasn't time to begin cooking.... Not yet. What was it she had been thinking about? Ah! the Solomonsons and the Capeses and the Bernards and the Carmels and the Lees. Would they talk of her and Trafford? It would be strange to go back to it all. Would they go back to it all? She found herself thinking intently of Trafford.

What a fine human being he was! And how touchingly human! The thoughts of his moments of irritation, his baffled silences, filled her with a wild passion of tenderness. She had disappointed him; all that life failed to satisfy him. Dear master of her life! what was it he needed? She too wasn't satisfied with life, but while she had been able to assuage herself with a perpetual series of petty excitements, theatres, new books and new people, meetings, movements, dinners, shows, he had grown to an immense discontent. He had most of the things men sought, wealth, respect, love, children.... So many men might have blunted their heart-ache with—adventures. There were pretty women, clever women, unoccupied women. She felt she wouldn't have minded— much—if it made him happy.... It was so wonderful he loved her still.... It wasn't that he lacked occupation; on the whole he overworked. His business interests were big and wide. Ought he to go into politics?

Why was it that the researches that had held him once, could hold him now no more? That was the real pity of it. Was she to blame for that? She couldn't state a case against herself, and yet she felt she was to blame. She had taken him away from those things, forced him to make money....

She sat chin on hand staring into the fire, the sock forgotten on her knee.

She could not weigh justice between herself and him. If he was unhappy it was her fault. She knew if he was unhappy it was no excuse that she had not known, had been misled, had a right to her own instincts and purposes. She had got to make him happy. But what was she to do, what was there for her to do?...

Only he could work out his own salvation, and until he had light, all she could do was to stand by him, help him, cease to irritate him, watch, wait. Anyhow she could at least mend his socks as well as possible, so that the threads would not chafe him....

She flashed to her feet. What was that?

It seemed to her she had heard the sound of a shot, and a quick brief wake of echoes. She looked across the icy waste of the river, and then up the tangled slopes of the mountain. Her heart was beating very fast. It must have been up there, and no doubt he had killed his beast. Some shadow of doubt she would not admit crossed that obvious suggestion.

This wilderness was making her as nervously responsive as a creature of the wild.

Came a second shot; this time there was no doubt of it. Then the desolate silence closed about her again.

She stood for a long time staring at the shrubby slopes that rose to the barren rock wilderness of the purple mountain crest. She sighed deeply at last, and set herself to make up the fire and prepare for the mid-day meal. Once far away across the river she heard the howl of a wolf.

Time seemed to pass very slowly that day. She found herself going repeatedly to the space between the day tent and the sleeping hut from which she could see the stunted wood that had swallowed him up, and after what seemed a long hour her watch told her it was still only half-past twelve. And the fourth or fifth time that she went to look out she was set atremble again by the sound of a third shot. And then at regular intervals out of that distant brown purple jumble of thickets against the snow came two more shots. "Something has happened," she said, "something has happened," and stood rigid. Then she became active, seized the rifle that was always at hand when she was alone, fired into the sky and stood listening.

Prompt come an answering shot.

"He wants me," said Marjorie. "Something——Perhaps he has killed something too big to bring!"

She was for starting at once, and then remembered this was not the way of the wilderness.

She thought and moved very rapidly. Her mind catalogued possible requirements, rifle, hunting knife, the oilskin bag with matches, and some chunks of dry paper, the rucksack—and he would be hungry. She took a saucepan and a huge chunk of cheese and biscuit. Then a brandy flask is sometimes handy—one never knows. Though nothing was wrong, of course. Needles and stout thread, and some cord. Snowshoes. A waterproof cloak could be easily carried. Her light hatchet for wood. She cast about to see if there was anything else. She had almost forgotten cartridges—and a revolver. Nothing more. She kicked a stray brand or so into the fire, put on some more wood, damped the fire with an armful of snow to make it last longer, and set out towards the willows into which he had vanished.

There was a rustling and snapping of branches as she pushed her way through the bushes, a little stir that died insensibly into quiet again; and then the camping place became very still....

Scarcely a sound occurred, except for the little shuddering and stirring of the fire, and the reluctant, infrequent drip from the icicles along the sunny edge of the log hut roof. About one o'clock the amber sunshine faded out altogether, a veil of clouds thickened and became greyly ominous, and a little after two the first flakes of a snowstorm fell hissing into the fire. A wind rose and drove the multiplying snowflakes in whirls and eddies before it. The icicles ceased to drip, but one or two broke and fell with a weak tinkling. A deep soughing, a shuddering groaning of trees and shrubs, came ever and again out of the ravine, and the powdery snow blew like puffs of smoke from the branches.

By four the fire was out, and the snow was piling high in the darkling twilight against tent and hut....

Trafford's trail led Marjorie through the thicket of dwarf willows and down to the gully of the rivulet which they had called Marjorie Trickle; it had long since become a trough of snow-covered rotten ice; the trail crossed this and, turning sharply uphill, went on until it was clear of shrubs and trees, and in the windy open of the upper slopes it crossed a ridge and came over the lip of a large desolate valley with slopes of ice and icy snow. Here she spent some time in following his loops back on the homeward trail before she saw what was manifestly the final trail running far away out across the snow, with the spoor of the lynx, a lightly-dotted line, to the right of it. She followed this suggestion of the trail, put on her snowshoes, and shuffled her way across this valley, which opened as she proceeded. She hoped that over the ridge she would find Trafford, and scanned the sky for the faintest discolouration of a fire, but there was none. That seemed odd to her, but the wind was in her face, and perhaps it beat the smoke down. Then as her eyes scanned the hummocky ridge ahead, she saw something, something very intent and still, that brought her heart into her mouth. It was a big, grey wolf, standing with back haunched and head down, watching and winding something beyond there, out of sight.

Marjorie had an instinctive fear of wild animals, and it still seemed dreadful to her that they should go at large, uncaged. She suddenly wanted Trafford violently, wanted him by her side. Also she thought of leaving the trail, going back to the bushes. She had to take herself in hand. In the wastes one did not fear wild beasts. One had no fear of them. But why not fire a shot to let him know she was near?

The beast flashed round with an animal's instantaneous change of pose, and looked at her. For a couple of seconds, perhaps, woman and brute regarded one another across a quarter of a mile of snowy desolation.

Suppose it came towards her!

She would fire—and she would fire at it. She made a guess at the range and aimed very carefully. She saw the snow fly two yards ahead of the grisly shape, and then in an instant it had vanished over the crest.

She reloaded, and stood for a moment waiting for Trafford's answer. No answer came. "Queer!" she whispered, "queer!"—and suddenly such a horror of anticipation assailed her that she started running and floundering through the snow to escape it. Twice she called his name, and once she just stopped herself from firing a shot.

Over the ridge she would find him. Surely she would find him over the ridge.She found herself among rocks, and there was a beaten and trampled place where Trafford must have waited and crouched. Then on and down a slope of tumbled boulders. There came a patch where he had either thrown himself down or fallen.

It seemed to her he must have been running....

Suddenly, a hundred feet or so away, she saw a patch of violently disturbed snow—snow stained a dreadful colour, a snow of scarlet crystals! Three strides and Trafford was in sight.

She had a swift conviction he was dead. He was lying in a crumpled attitude on a patch of snow between convergent rocks, and the lynx, a mass of blood smeared silvery fur, was in some way mixed up with him. She saw as she came nearer that the snow was disturbed round about them, and discoloured copiously, yellow widely, and in places bright red, with congealed and frozen blood. She felt no fear now, and no emotion; all her mind was engaged with the clear, bleak perception of the fact before her. She did not care to call to him again. His head was hidden by the lynx's body, it was as if he was burrowing underneath the creature; his legs were twisted about each other in a queer, unnatural attitude.

Then, as she dropped off a boulder, and came nearer, Trafford moved. A hand came out and gripped the rifle beside him; he suddenly lifted a dreadful face, horribly scarred and torn, and crimson with frozen blood; he pushed the grey beast aside, rose on an elbow, wiped his sleeve across his eyes, stared at her, grunted, and flopped forward. He had fainted.

She was now as clear-minded and as self-possessed as a woman in a shop. In another moment she was kneeling by his side. She saw, by the position of his knife and the huge rip in the beast's body, that he had stabbed the lynx to death as it clawed his head; he must have shot and wounded it and then fallen upon it. His knitted cap was torn to ribbons, and hung upon his neck. Also his leg was manifestly injured; how, she could not tell. It was chiefly evident he must freeze if he lay here. It seemed to her that perhaps he had pulled the dead brute over him to protect his torn skin from the extremity of cold. The lynx was already rigid, its clumsy paws asprawl—the torn skin and clot upon Trafford's face was stiff as she put her hands about his head to raise him. She turned him over on his back—how heavy he seemed!—and forced brandy between his teeth. Then, after a moment's hesitation, she poured a little brandy on his wounds.

She glanced at his leg, which was surely broken, and back at his face. Then she gave him more brandy and his eyelids flickered. He moved his hand weakly. "The blood," he said, "kept getting in my eyes."

She gave him brandy once again, wiped his face and glanced at his leg. Something ought to be done to that she thought. But things must be done in order.

She stared up at the darkling sky with its grey promise of snow, and down the slopes of the mountain. Clearly they must stay the night here. They were too high for wood among these rocks, but three or four hundred yards below there were a number of dwarfed fir trees. She had brought an axe, so that a fire was possible. Should she go back to camp and get the tent?

Trafford was trying to speak again. "I got——" he said.

"Yes?"

"Got my leg in that crack. Damn—damned nuisance."

Was he able to advise her? She looked at him, and then perceived she must bind up his head and face. She knelt behind him and raised his head on her knee. She had a thick silk neck muffler, and this she supplemented by a band she cut and tore from her inner vest. She bound this, still warm from her body, about him, wrapped her cloak round him. The next thing was a fire. Five yards away, perhaps, a great mass of purple gabbro hung over a patch of nearly snowless moss. A hummock to the westward offered shelter from the weakly bitter wind, the icy draught, that was soughing down the valley. Always in Labrador, if you can, you camp against a rock surface; it shelters you from the wind, reflects your fire, guards your back.

"Rag!" she said.

"Rotten hole," said Trafford.

"What?" she cried sharply.

"Got you in a rotten hole," he said. "Eh?"

"Listen," she said, and shook his shoulder. "Look! I want to get you up against that rock."

"Won't make much difference," said Trafford, and opened his eyes. "Where?" he asked.

"There."

He remained quite quiet for a second perhaps. "Listen to me," he said. "Go back to camp."

"Yes," she said.

"Go back to camp. Make a pack of all the strongest food—strenthin'—strengthrin' food—you know?" He seemed troubled to express himself.

"Yes," she said.

"Down the river. Down—down. Till you meet help."

"Leave you?"

He nodded his head and winced.

"You're always plucky," he said. "Look facts in the face. Kiddies. Thought it over while you were coming." A tear oozed from his eye. "Not be a fool, Madge. Kiss me good-bye. Not be a fool. I'm done. Kids."

She stared at him and her spirit was a luminous mist of tears. "You old coward," she said in his ear, and kissed the little patch of rough and bloody cheek beneath his eye. Then she knelt up beside him. "I'm boss now, old man," she said. "I want to get you to that place there under the rock. If I drag, can you help?"

He answered obstinately: "You'd better go."

"I'll make you comfortable first," she answered, "anyhow."

He made an enormous effort, and then with her quick help and with his back to her knee, had raised himself on his elbows.

"And afterwards?" he asked.

"Build a fire."

"Wood?"

"Down there."

"Two bits of wood tied on my leg—splints. Then I can drag myself. See? Like a blessed old walrus."

He smiled, and she kissed his bandaged face again.

"Else it hurts," he apologized, "more than I can stand."

She stood up again, thought, put his rifle and knife to his hand for fear of that lurking wolf, abandoning her own rifle with an effort, and went striding and leaping from rock to rock towards the trees below. She made the chips fly, and was presently towing three venerable pine dwarfs, bumping over rock and crevice, back to Trafford. She flung them down, stood for a moment bright and breathless, then set herself to hack off the splints he needed from the biggest stem. "Now," she said, coming to him.

"A fool," he remarked, "would have made the splints down there. You're—good, Marjorie."

She lugged his leg out straight, put it into the natural and least painful pose, padded it with moss and her torn handkerchief, and bound it up. As she did so a handful of snowflakes came whirling about them. She was now braced up to every possibility. "It never rains," she said grimly, "but it pours," and went on with her bone-setting. He was badly weakened by pain and shock, and once he swore at her sharply. "Sorry," he said.

She rolled him over on his chest, and left him to struggle to the shelter of the rock while she went for more wood.

The sky alarmed her. The mountains up the valley were already hidden by driven rags of slaty snowstorms. This time she found a longer but easier path for dragging her boughs and trees; she determined she would not start the fire until nightfall, nor waste any time in preparing food until then. There were dead boughs for kindling—more than enough. It was snowing quite fast by the time she got up to him with her second load, and a premature twilight already obscured and exaggerated the rocks and mounds about her. She gave some of her cheese to Trafford, and gnawed some herself on her way down to the wood again. She regretted that she had brought neither candles nor lantern, because then she might have kept on until the cold of night stopped her, and she reproached herself bitterly because she had brought no tea. She could forgive herself the lantern, she had never expected to be out after dark, but the tea was inexcusable. She muttered self-reproaches while she worked like two men among the trees, panting puffs of mist that froze upon her lips and iced the knitted wool that covered her chin. Why don't they teach a girl to handle an axe?...

When at last the wolfish cold of the Labrador night had come, it found Trafford and Marjorie seated almost warmly on a bed of pine boughs between the sheltering dark rock behind and a big but well husbanded fire in front, drinking a queer-tasting but not unsavory soup of lynx-flesh, that she had fortified with the remainder of the brandy. Then they tried roast lynx and ate a little, and finished with some scraps of cheese and deep draughts of hot water. Then—oh Tyburnia and Chelsea and all that is becoming!—they smoked Trafford's pipe for alternate minutes, and Marjorie found great comfort in it.

The snowstorm poured incessantly out of the darkness to become flakes of burning fire in the light of the flames, flakes that vanished magically, but it only reached them and wetted them in occasional gusts. What did it matter for the moment if the dim snow-heaps rose and rose about them? A glorious fatigue, an immense self-satisfaction possessed Marjorie; she felt that they had both done well.

"I am not afraid of to-morrow now," she said at last—a thought matured. "No!"

Trafford had the pipe and did not speak for a moment. "Nor I," he said at last. "Very likely we'll get through with it." He added after a pause: "I thought I was done for. A man—loses heart. After a loss of blood."

"The leg's better?"

"Hot as fire." His humour hadn't left him. "It's a treat," he said. "The hottest thing in Labrador."

"I've been a good squaw this time, old man?" she asked suddenly.

He seemed not to hear her; then his lips twitched and he made a feeble movement for her hand. "I cursed you," he said....

She slept, but on a spring as it were, lest the fire should fall. She replenished it with boughs, tucked in the half-burnt logs, and went to sleep again. Then it seemed to her that some invisible hand was pouring a thin spirit on the flames that made them leap and crackle and spread north and south until they filled the heavens. Her eyes were open and the snowstorm overpast, leaving the sky clear, and all the westward heaven alight with the trailing, crackling, leaping curtains of the Aurora, brighter than she had ever seen them before. Quite clearly visible beyond the smoulder of the fire, a wintry waste of rock and snow, boulder beyond boulder, passed into a dun obscurity. The mountain to the right of them lay long and white and stiff, a shrouded death. All earth was dead and waste and nothing, and the sky alive and coldly marvellous, signalling and astir. She watched the changing, shifting colours, and they made her think of the gathering banners of inhuman hosts, the stir and marshalling of icy giants for ends stupendous and indifferent to all the trivial impertinence of man's existence....

That night the whole world of man seemed small and shallow and insecure to her, beyond comparison. One came, she thought, but just a little way out of its warm and sociable cities hither, and found this homeless wilderness; one pricked the thin appearances of life with microscope or telescope and came to an equal strangeness. All the pride and hope of human life goes to and fro in a little shell of air between this ancient globe of rusty nickel-steel and the void of space; faint specks we are within a film; we quiver between the atom and the infinite, being hardly more substantial than the glow within an oily skin that drifts upon the water. The wonder and the riddle of it! Here she and Trafford were! Phantasmal shapes of unsubstantial fluid thinly skinned against evaporation and wrapped about with woven wool and the skins of beasts, that yet reflected and perceived, suffered and sought to understand; that held a million memories, framed thoughts that plumbed the deeps of space and time,—and another day of snow or icy wind might leave them just scattered bones and torn rags gnawed by a famishing wolf!...

She felt a passionate desire to pray....

She glanced at Trafford beside her, and found him awake and staring. His face was very pale and strange in that livid, flickering light. She would have spoken, and then she saw his lips were moving, and something, something she did not understand, held her back from doing so.

§ 7

The bleak, slow dawn found Marjorie intently busy. She had made up the fire, boiled water and washed and dressed Trafford's wounds, and made another soup of lynx. But Trafford had weakened in the night, the stuff nauseated him, he refused it and tried to smoke and was sick, and then sat back rather despairfully after a second attempt to persuade her to leave him there to die. This failure of his spirit distressed her and a little astonished her, but it only made her more resolute to go through with her work. She had awakened cold, stiff and weary, but her fatigue vanished with movement; she toiled for an hour replenishing her pile of fuel, made up the fire, put his gun ready to his hand, kissed him, abused him lovingly for the trouble he gave her until his poor torn face lit in response, and then parting on a note of cheerful confidence set out to return to the hut. She found the way not altogether easy to make out, wind and snow had left scarcely a trace of their tracks, and her mind was full of the stores she must bring and the possibility of moving him nearer to the hut. She was startled to see by the fresh, deep spoor along the ridge how near the wolf had dared approach them in the darkness....

Ever and again Marjorie had to halt and look back to get her direction right. As it was she came through the willow scrub nearly half a mile above the hut, and had to follow the steep bank of the frozen river down. At one place she nearly slipped upon an icy slope of rock.

One possibility she did not dare to think of during that time; a blizzard now would cut her off absolutely from any return to Trafford. Short of that she believed she could get through.

Her quick mind was full of all she had to do. At first she had thought chiefly of his immediate necessities, of food and some sort of shelter. She had got a list of things in her head—meat extract, bandages, corrosive sublimate by way of antiseptic, brandy, a tin of beef, some bread and so forth; she went over that several times to be sure of it, and then for a time she puzzled about a tent. She thought she could manage a bale of blankets on her back, and that she could rig a sleeping tent for herself and Trafford with one and some bent sticks. The big tent would be too much to strike and shift. And then her mind went on to a bolder enterprise, which was to get him home. The nearer she could bring him to the log hut, the nearer they would be to supplies. She cast about for some sort of sledge. The snow was too soft and broken for runners, especially among the trees, but if she could get a flat of smooth wood she thought she might be able to drag him. She decided to try the side of her bunk. She could easily get that off. She would have, of course, to run it edgewise through the thickets and across the ravine, but after that she would have almost clear going until she reached the steep place of broken rocks within two hundred yards of him. The idea of a sledge grew upon her, and she planned to nail a rope along the edge and make a kind of harness for herself.

She found the camping-place piled high with drifted snow, which had invaded tent and hut, and that some beast, a wolverine she guessed, had been into the hut, devoured every candle-end and the uppers of Trafford's well-greased second boots, and had then gone to the corner of the store shed and clambered up to the stores. She made no account of its depredations there, but set herself to make a sledge and get her supplies together. There was a gleam of sunshine, but she did not like the look of the sky, and she was horribly afraid of what might be happening to Trafford. She carried her stuff through the wood and across the ravine, and returned for her improvised sledge. She was still struggling with that among the trees when it began to snow again.

It was hard then not to be frantic in her efforts. As it was, she packed her stuff so loosely on the planking that she had to repack it, and she started without putting on her snowshoes, and floundered fifty yards before she discovered that omission. The snow was now falling fast, darkling the sky and hiding everything but objects close at hand, and she had to use all her wits to determine her direction; she knew she must go down a long slope and then up to the ridge, and it came to her as a happy inspiration that if she bore to the left she might strike some recognizable vestige of her morning's trail. She had read of people walking in circles when they have no light or guidance, and that troubled her until she bethought herself of the little compass on her watch chain. By that she kept her direction. She wished very much she had timed herself across the waste, so that she could tell when she approached the ridge.

Soon her back and shoulders were aching violently, and the rope across her chest was tugging like some evil-tempered thing. But she did not dare to rest. The snow was now falling thick and fast, the flakes traced white spirals and made her head spin, so that she was constantly falling away to the south-westward and then correcting herself by the compass. She tried to think how this zig-zagging might affect her course, but the snow whirls confused her mind and a growing anxiety would not let her pause to think. She felt blinded; it seemed to be snowing inside her eyes so that she wanted to rub them. Soon the ground must rise to the ridge, she told herself; it must surely rise. Then the sledge came bumping at her heels and she perceived she was going down hill. She consulted the compass, and she found she was facing south. She turned sharply to the right again. The snowfall became a noiseless, pitiless torture to sight and mind.

The sledge behind her struggled to hold her back, and the snow balled under her snowshoes. She wanted to stop and rest, take thought, sit for a moment. She struggled with herself and kept on. She tried walking with shut eyes, and tripped and came near sprawling. "Oh God!" she cried, "oh God!" too stupefied for more articulate prayers.

Would the rise of the ground to the ribs of rock never come?

A figure, black and erect, stood in front of her suddenly, and beyond appeared a group of black, straight antagonists. She staggered on towards them, gripping her rifle with some muddled idea of defence, and in another moment she was brushing against the branches of a stunted fir, which shed thick lumps of snow upon her feet. What trees were these? Had she ever passed any trees? No! There were no trees on her way to Trafford....

She began whimpering like a tormented child. But even as she wept she turned her sledge about to follow the edge of the wood. She was too much downhill, she thought and she must bear up again.

She left the trees behind, made an angle uphill to the right, and was presently among trees again. Again she left them and again came back to them. She screamed with anger at them and twitched her sledge away. She wiped at the snowstorm with her arm as though she would wipe it away. She wanted to stamp on the universe....

And she ached, she ached....

Something caught her eye ahead, something that gleamed; it was exactly like a long, bare rather pinkish bone standing erect on the ground. Just because it was strange and queer she ran forward to it. Then as she came nearer she perceived it was a streak of barked trunk; a branch had been torn off a pine tree and the bark stripped down to the root. And then her foot hit against a freshly hewn stump, and then came another, poking its pinkish wounds above the snow. And there were chips! This filled her with wonder. Some one had been cutting wood! There must be Indians or trappers near, she thought, and then realized the wood-cutter could be none other than herself.

She turned to the right and saw the rocks rising steeply close at hand. "Oh Rag!" she cried, and fired her rifle in the air.

Ten seconds, twenty seconds, and then so loud and near it amazed her, came his answering shot. It sounded like the hillside bursting.

In another moment she had discovered the trail she had made overnight and that morning by dragging firewood. It was now a shallow soft white trench. Instantly her despair and fatigue had gone from her. Should she take a load of wood with her? she asked herself, in addition to the weight behind her, and had a better idea. She would unload and pile her stuff here, and bring him down on the sledge closer to the wood. She looked about and saw two rocks that diverged with a space between. She flashed schemes. She would trample the snow hard and flat, put her sledge on it, pile boughs and make a canopy of blanket overhead and behind. Then a fire in front.

She saw her camp admirable. She tossed her provisions down and ran up the broad windings of her pine-tree trail to Trafford, with the unloaded sledge bumping behind her. She ran as lightly as though she had done nothing that day.

She found him markedly recovered, weak and quiet, with snow drifting over his feet, his rifle across his knees, and his pipe alight. "Back already," he said, "but——"

He hesitated. "No grub?"

She knelt over him, gave his rough unshaven cheek a swift kiss, and very rapidly explained her plan.

§ 8

In three days' time they were back at the hut, and the last two days they wore blue spectacles because of the mid-day glare of the sunlit snow.

It amazed Marjorie to discover as she lay awake in the camp on the edge of the ravine close to the hut to which she had lugged Trafford during the second day, that she was deeply happy. It was preposterous that she should be so, but those days of almost despairful stress were irradiated now by a new courage. She was doing this thing, against all Labrador and the snow-driving wind that blew from the polar wilderness, she was winning. It was a great discovery to her that hardship and effort almost to the breaking-point could ensue in so deep a satisfaction. She lay and thought how deep and rich life had become for her, as though in all this effort and struggle some unsuspected veil had been torn away. She perceived again, but now with no sense of desolation, that same infinite fragility of life which she had first perceived when she had watched the Aurora Borealis flickering up the sky. Beneath that realization and carrying it, as a river flood may carry scum, was a sense of herself as something deeper, greater, more enduring than mountain or wilderness or sky, or any of those monstrous forms of nature that had dwarfed her physical self to nothingness.

She had a persuasion of self detachment and illumination, and withal of self-discovery. She saw her life of time and space for what it was. Away in London the children, with the coldest of noses and the gayest of spirits, would be scampering about their bedrooms in the mild morning sunlight of a London winter; Elsie, the parlourmaid, would be whisking dexterous about the dining-room, the bacon would be cooking and the coffee-mill at work, the letters of the morning delivery perhaps just pattering into the letter-box, and all the bright little household she had made, with all the furniture she had arranged, all the characteristic decoration she had given it, all the clever convenient arrangements, would be getting itself into action for another day—and it wasn't herself! It was the extremest of her superficiality.

She had come out of all that, and even so it seemed she had come out of herself; this weary woman lying awake on the balsam boughs with a brain cleared by underfeeding and this continuous arduous bath of toil in snow-washed, frost cleansed, starry air, this, too, was no more than a momentarily clarified window for her unknown and indefinable reality. What was that reality? what was she herself? She became interested in framing an answer to that, and slipped down from the peace of soul she had attained. Her serenity gave way to a reiteration of this question, reiterations increasing and at last oppressing like the snowflakes of a storm, perpetual whirling repetitions that at last confused her and hid the sky....

She fell asleep....

§ 9

With their return to the hut, Marjorie had found herself encountering a new set of urgencies. In their absence that wretched little wolverine had found great plenty and happiness in the tent and store-shed; its traces were manifest nearly everywhere, and it had particularly assailed the candles, after a destructive time among the frozen caribou beef. It had clambered up on the packages of sardines and jumped thence on to a sloping pole that it could claw along into the frame of the roof. She rearranged the packages, but that was no good. She could not leave Trafford in order to track the brute down, and for a night or so she could not think of any way of checking its depredations. It came each night…. Trafford kept her close at home. She had expected that when he was back in his bunk, secure and warm, he would heal rapidly, but instead he suddenly developed all the symptoms of a severe feverish cold, and his scars, which had seemed healing, became flushed and ugly-looking. Moreover, there was something wrong with his leg, an ominous ache that troubled her mind. Every woman, she decided, ought to know how to set a bone. He was unable to sleep by reason of these miseries, though very desirous of doing so. He became distressingly weak and inert, he ceased to care for food, and presently he began ta talk to himself with a complete disregard of her presence. Hourly she regretted her ignorance of medicine that left her with no conceivable remedy for all the aching and gnawing that worried and weakened him, except bathing with antiseptics and a liberal use of quinine.

And his face became strange to her, for over his flushed and sunken cheeks, under the raw spaces of the scar a blond beard bristled and grew. Presently, Trafford was a bearded man.

Incidentally, however, she killed the wolverine by means of a trap of her own contrivance, a loaded rifle with a bait of what was nearly her last candles, rigged to the trigger.

But this loss of the candles brought home to them the steady lengthening of the nights. Scarcely seven hours of day remained now in the black, cold grip of the darkness. And through those seventeen hours of chill aggression they had no light but the red glow of the stove. She had to close the door of the hut and bar every chink and cranny against the icy air, that became at last a murderous, freezing wind. Not only did she line the hut with every scrap of skin and paper she could obtain, but she went out with the spade toiling for three laborious afternoons in piling and beating snow against the outer frame. And now it was that Trafford talked at last, talked with something of the persistence of delirium, and she sat and listened hour by hour, silently, for he gave no heed to her or to anything she might say. He talked, it seemed, to God….

Darkness about a sullen glow of red, and a voice speaking.

The voice of a man, fevered and in pain, wounded and amidst hardship and danger, struggling with the unrelenting riddle of his being. Ever and again when a flame leapt she would see his face, haggard, bearded, changed, and yet infinitely familiar.

His voice varied, now high and clear, now mumbling, now vexed and expostulating, now rich with deep feeling, now fagged and slow; his matter varied, too; now he talked like one who is inspired, and now like one lost and confused, stupidly repeating phrases, going back upon a misleading argument, painfully, laboriously beginning over and over again. Marjorie sat before the stove watching it burn and sink, replenishing it, preparing food, and outside the bitter wind moaned and blew the powdery snow before it, and the shortening interludes of pallid, diffused daylight which pass for days in such weather, came and went. Intense cold had come now with leaden snowy days and starless nights.

Sometimes his speech filled her mind, seemed to fill all her world; sometimes she ceased to listen, following thoughts of her own. Sometimes she dozed; sometimes she awakened from sleep to find him talking. But slowly she realized a thread in his discourse, a progress and development.

Sometimes he talked of his early researches, and then he would trace computations with his hands as if he were using a blackboard, and became distressed to remember what he had written. Sometimes he would be under the claws of the lynx again, and fighting for his eyes. "Ugh!" he said, "keep those hind legs still. Keep your hind legs still! Knife? Knife? Ah! got it. Gu—u—u, you Beast!"

But the gist of his speech was determined by the purpose of his journey to Labrador. At last he was reviewing his life and hers, and all that their life might signify, even as he determined to do. She began to perceive that whatever else drifted into his mind and talk, this recurred and grew, that he returned to the conclusion he had reached, and not to the beginning of the matter, and went on from that....

"You see," he said, "our lives are nothing—nothing in themselves. I know that; I've never had any doubts of that. We individuals just pick up a mixed lot of things out of the powers that begat us, and lay them down again presently a little altered, that's all—heredities, traditions, the finger nails of my grandfather, a great-aunt's lips, the faith of a sect, the ideas of one's time. We live and then we die, and the threads run, dispersing this way and that. To make other people again. Whatever's immortal isn't that, our looks or our habits, our thoughts or our memories—just the shapes, these are, of one immortal stuff.... One immortal stuff."...

The voice died away as if he was baffled. Then it resumed.

"But we ought to partake of immortality; that's my point. We ought to partake of immortality.

"I mean we're like the little elements in a magnet; ought not to lie higgledy-piggledy, ought to point the same way, be polarized——Something microcosmic, you know, ought to be found in a man.

"Analogies run away with one. Suppose the bar isn't magnetized yet! Suppose purpose has to come; suppose the immortal stuff isn't yet, isn't being but struggling to be. Struggling to be.... Gods! that morning! When the child was born! And afterwards she was there—with a smile on her lips, and a little flushed and proud—as if nothing had happened so very much out of the way. Nothing so wonderful. And we had another life besides our own!..."

Afterwards he came back to that. "That was a good image," he said, "something trying to exist, which isn't substance, doesn't belong to space or time, something stifled and enclosed, struggling to get through. Just confused birth cries, eyes that hardly see, deaf ears, poor little thrusting hands. A thing altogether blind at first, a twitching and thrusting of protoplasm under the waters, and then the plants creeping up the beaches, the insects and reptiles on the margins of the rivers, beasts with a flicker of light in their eyes answering the sun. And at last, out of the long interplay of desire and fear, an ape, an ape that stared and wondered, and scratched queer pictures on a bone...."

He lapsed into silent thought for a time, and Marjorie glanced at his dim face in the shadows.

"I say nothing of ultimates," he said at last.

He repeated that twice before his thoughts would flow again.

"This is as much as I see, in time as I know it and space as I know it—something struggling to exist. It's true to the end of my limits. What can I say beyond that? It struggles to exist, becomes conscious, becomes now conscious of itself. That is where I come in, as a part of it. Above the beast in me is that—the desire to know better, to know—beautifully, and to transmit my knowledge. That's all there is in life for me beyond food and shelter and tidying up. This Being—opening its eyes, listening, trying to comprehend. Every good thing in man is that;—looking and making pictures, listening and making songs, making philosophies and sciences, trying new powers, bridge and engine, spark and gun. At the bottom of my soul, that. We began with bone-scratching. We're still—near it. I am just a part of this beginning—mixed with other things. Every book, every art, every religion is that, the attempt to understand and express—mixed with other things. Nothing else matters, nothing whatever. I tell you——Nothing whatever!

"I've always believed that. All my life I've believed that.

"Only I've forgotten."

"Every man with any brains believes that at the bottom of his heart. Only he gets busy and forgets. He goes shooting lynxes and breaks his leg. Odd, instinctive, brutal thing to do—to go tracking down a lynx to kill it! I grant you that, Marjorie. I grant you that."

"Grant me what?" she cried, startled beyond measure to hear herself addressed.

"Grant you that it is rather absurd to go hunting a lynx. And what big paws it has—disproportionately big! I wonder if that's an adaptation to snow. Tremendous paws they are.... But the real thing, I was saying, the real thing is to get knowledge, and express it. All things lead up to that. Civilization, social order, just for that. Except for that, all the life of man, all his affairs, his laws and police, his morals and manners—nonsense, nonsense, nonsense. Lynx hunts! Just ways of getting themselves mauled and clawed perhaps—into a state of understanding. Who knows?..."

His voice became low and clear.

"Understanding spreading like a dawn....

"Logic and language, clumsy implements, but rising to our needs, rising to our needs, thought clarified, enriched, reaching out to every man alive—some day—presently—touching every man alive, harmonizing acts and plans, drawing men into gigantic co-operations, tremendous co-operations....

"Until man shall stand upon this earth as upon a footstool and reach out his hand among the stars....

"And then I went into the rubber market, and spent seven years of my life driving shares up and down and into a net!... Queer game indeed! Stupid ass Behrens was—at bottom....

"There's a flaw in it somewhere...."

He came back to that several times before he seemed able to go on from it.

"There is a collective mind," he said, "a growing general consciousness—growing clearer. Something put me away from that, but I know it. My work, my thinking, was a part of it. That's why I was so mad about Behrens."

"Behrens?"

"Of course. He'd got a twist, a wrong twist. It makes me angry now. It will take years, it will eat up some brilliant man to clean up after Behrens——"

"Yes, but the point is"—his voice became acute—"why did I go making money and let Behrens in? Why generally and in all sorts of things does Behrens come in?..."

He was silent for a long time, and then he began to answer himself. "Of course," he said, "I said it—or somebody said it—about this collective mind being mixed with other things. It's something arising out of life—not the common stuff of life. An exhalation.... It's like the little tongues of fire that came at Pentecost.... Queer how one comes drifting back to these images. Perhaps I shall die a Christian yet.... The other Christians won't like me if I do. What was I saying?... It's what I reach up to, what I desire shall pervade me, not what I am. Just as far as I give myself purely to knowledge, to making feeling and thought clear in my mind and words, to the understanding and expression of the realities and relations of life, just so far do I achieve Salvation.... Salvation!...

"I wonder, is Salvation the same for every one? Perhaps for one man Salvation is research and thought, and for another expression in art, and for another nursing lepers. Provided he does it in the spirit. He has to do it in the spirit...."

There came a silence as though some difficulty baffled him, and he was feeling back to get his argument again.

"This flame that arises out of life, that redeems life from purposeless triviality, isn't life. Let me get hold of that. That's a point. That's a very important point."

Something had come to him.

"I've never talked of this to Marjorie. I've lived with her nine years and more, and never talked of religion. Not once. That's so queer of us. Any other couple in any other time would have talked religion no end.... People ought to."

Then he stuck out an argumentative hand. "You see, Marjorie is life," he said.

"She took me."

He spoke slowly, as though he traced things carefully.

"Before I met her I suppose I wasn't half alive. No! Yet I don't remember I felt particularly incomplete. Women were interesting, of course; they excited me at times, that girl at Yonkers!—H'm. I stuck to my work. It was fine work, I forget half of it now, the half-concealed intimations I mean—queer how one forgets!—but I know I felt my way to wide, deep things. It was like exploring caves—monstrous, limitless caves. Such caves!... Very still—underground. Wonderful and beautiful.... They're lying there now for other men to seek. Other men will find them.... Then she came, as though she was taking possession. The beauty of her, oh! the life and bright eagerness, and the incompatibility! That's the riddle! I've loved her always. When she came to my arms it seemed to me the crown of life. Caves indeed! Old caves! Nothing else seemed to matter. But something did. All sorts of things did. I found that out soon enough. And when that first child was born. That for a time was supreme.... Yes—she's the quintessence of life, the dear greed of her, the appetite, the clever appetite for things. She grabs. She's so damned clever! The light in her eyes! Her quick sure hands!... Only my work was crowded out of my life and ended, and she didn't seem to feel it, she didn't seem to mind it. There was a sort of disregard. Disregard. As though all that didn't really matter...."

"My dear!" whispered Marjorie unheeded. She wanted to tell him it mattered now, mattered supremely, but she knew he had no ears for her.

His voice flattened. "It's perplexing," he said. "The two different things."

Then suddenly he cried out harshly: "I ought never to have married her—never, never! I had my task. I gave myself to her. Oh! the high immensities, the great and terrible things open to the mind of man! And we breed children and live in littered houses and play with our food and chatter, chatter, chatter. Oh, the chatter of my life! The folly! The women with their clothes. I can hear them rustle now, whiff the scent of it! The scandals—as though the things they did with themselves and each other mattered a rap; the little sham impromptu clever things, the trying to keep young—and underneath it all that continual cheating, cheating, cheating, damning struggle for money!...

"Marjorie, Marjorie, Marjorie! Why is she so good and no better! Why wasn't she worth it altogether?...

"No! I don't want to go on with it any more—ever. I want to go back.

"I want my life over again, and to go back.

"I want research, and the spirit of research that has died in me, and that still, silent room of mine again, that room, as quiet as a cell, and the toil that led to light. Oh! the coming of that light, the uprush of discovery, the solemn joy as the generalization rises like a sun upon the facts—floods them with a common meaning. That is what I want. That is what I have always wanted....

"Give me my time oh God! again; I am sick of this life I have chosen. I am sick of it! This—busy death! Give me my time again.... Why did you make me, and then waste me like this? Why are we made for folly upon folly? Folly! and brains made to scale high heaven, smeared into the dust! Into the dust, into the dust. Dust!..."

He passed into weak, wandering repetitions of disconnected sentences, that died into whispers and silence, and Marjorie watched him and listened to him, and waited with a noiseless dexterity upon his every need.

§ 11

One day, she did not know what day, for she had lost count of the days, Marjorie set the kettle to boil and opened the door of the hut to look out, and the snow was ablaze with diamonds, and the air was sweet and still. It occurred to her that it would be well to take Trafford out into that brief brightness. She looked at him and found his eyes upon the sunlight quiet and rather wondering eyes.

"Would you like to get out into that?" she asked abruptly.

"Yes," he said, and seemed disposed to get up.

"You've got a broken leg," she cried, to arrest his movement, and he looked at her and answered: "Of course—I forgot."

She was all atremble that he should recognize her and speak to her. She pulled her rude old sledge alongside his bunk, and kissed him, and showed him how to shift and drop himself upon the plank. She took him in her arms and lowered him. He helped weakly but understandingly, and she wrapped him up warmly on the planks and lugged him out and built up a big fire at his feet, wondering, but as yet too fearful to rejoice, at the change that had come to him.

He said no more, but his eyes watched her move about with a kind of tired curiosity. He smiled for a time at the sun, and shut his eyes, and still faintly smiling, lay still. She had a curious fear that if she tried to talk to him this new lucidity would vanish again. She went about the business of the morning, glancing at him ever and again, until suddenly the calm of his upturned face smote her, and she ran to him and crouched down to him between hope and a terrible fear, and found that he was sleeping, and breathing very lightly, sleeping with the deep unconsciousness of a child....

When he awakened the sun was red in the west. His eyes met hers, and he seemed a little puzzled.

"I've been sleeping, Madge?" he said.

She nodded.

"And dreaming? I've a vague sort of memory of preaching and preaching in a kind of black, empty place, where there wasn't anything.... A fury of exposition... a kind of argument.... I say!—Is there such a thing in the world as a new-laid egg—and some bread-and-butter?"

He seemed to reflect. "Of course," he said, "I broke my leg. Gollys! I thought that beast was going to claw my eyes out. Lucky, Madge, it didn't get my eyes. It was just a chance it didn't."

He stared at her.

"I say," he said, "you've had a pretty rough time! How long has this been going on?"

He amazed her by rising himself on his elbow and sitting up.

"Your leg!" she cried.

He put his hand down and felt it. "Pretty stiff," he said. "You get me some food—there were some eggs, Madge, frozen new-laid, anyhow—and then we'll take these splints off and feel about a bit. Eh! why not? How did you get me out of that scrape, Madge? I thought I'd got to be froze as safe as eggs. (Those eggs ought to be all right, you know. If you put them on in a saucepan and wait until they boil.) I've a sort of muddled impression.... By Jove, Madge, you've had a time! I say you have had a time!"

His eyes, full of a warmth of kindliness she had not seen for long weeks, scrutinized her face. "I say!" he repeated, very softly.

All her strength went from her at his tenderness. "Oh, my dear," she wailed, kneeling at his side, "my dear, dear!" and still regardful of his leg, she yet contrived to get herself weeping into his coveted arms.

He regarded her, he held her, he patted her back! The infinite luxury to her! He'd come back. He'd come back to her.

"How long has it been?" he asked. "Poor dear! Poor dear! How long can it have been?"

<h3 style="text-align:center">§ 12</h3>

From that hour Trafford mended. He remained clear-minded, helpful, sustaining. His face healed daily. Marjorie had had to cut away great fragments of gangrenous frozen flesh, and he was clearly destined to have a huge scar over forehead and cheek, but in that pure, clear air, once the healing had begun it progressed swiftly. His leg had set, a little shorter than its fellow and with a lump in the middle of the shin, but it promised to be a good serviceable leg none the less. They examined it by the light of the stove with their heads together, and discussed when it would be wise to try it. How do doctors tell when a man may stand on his broken leg? She had a vague impression you must wait six weeks, but she could not remember why she fixed upon that time.

"It seems a decent interval," said Trafford. "We'll try it."

She had contrived a crutch for him against that momentous experiment, and he sat up in his bunk, pillowed up by a sack and her rugs, and whittled it smooth, and padded the fork with the skin of that slaughtered wolverine, poor victim of hunger!—while she knelt by the stove feeding it with logs, and gave him an account of their position.

"We're somewhere in the middle of December," she said, "somewhere between the twelfth and the fourteenth,—yes! I'm as out as that!—and I've handled the stores pretty freely. So did that little beast until I got him." She nodded at the skin in his hand. "I don't see myself shooting much now, and so far I've not been able to break the ice to fish. It's too much for me. Even if it isn't too late to fish. This book we've got describes barks and mosses, and that will help, but if we stick here until the birds and things come, we're going to be precious short. We may have to last right into July. I've plans—but it may come to that. We ought to ration all the regular stuff, and trust to luck for a feast. The rations!—I don't know what they'll come to."

"Right O," said Trafford admiring her capable gravity. "Let's ration."

"Marjorie," he asked abruptly, "are you sorry we came?"

Her answer came unhesitatingly. "No!"

"Nor I."

He paused. "I've found you out," he said. "Dear dirty living thing!... You are dirty, you know."

"I've found myself," she answered, thinking. "I feel as if I've never loved you until this hut. I suppose I have in my way——"

"Lugano," he suggested. "Don't let's forget good things, Marjorie. Oh! And endless times!"

"Oh, of course! As for that——! But now—now you're in my bones. We were just two shallow, pretty, young things—loving. It was sweet, dear—sweet as youth—but not this. Unkempt and weary—then one understands love. I suppose I am dirty. Think of it!

I've lugged you through the snow till my shoulders chafed and bled. I cried with pain, and kept on lugging——Oh, my dear! my dear!" He kissed her hair. "I've held you in my arms to keep you from freezing. (I'd have frozen myself first.) We've got to starve together perhaps before the end.... Dear, if I could make you, you should eat me.... I'm—I'm beginning to understand. I've had a light. I've begun to understand. I've begun to see what life has been for you, and how I've wasted—wasted."

"We've wasted!"

"No," she said, "it was I."

She sat back on the floor and regarded him. "You don't remember things you said— when you were delirious?"

"No," he answered. "What did I say?"

"Nothing?"

"Nothing clearly. What did I say?"

"It doesn't matter. No, indeed. Only you made me understand. You'd never have told me. You've always been a little weak with me there. But it's plain to me why we didn't keep our happiness, why we were estranged. If we go back alive, we go back—all that settled for good and all."

"What?"

"That discord. My dear, I've been a fool, selfish, ill-trained and greedy. We've both been floundering about, but I've been the mischief of it. Yes, I've been the trouble. Oh, it's had to be so. What are we women—half savages, half pets, unemployed things of greed and desire—and suddenly we want all the rights and respect of souls! I've had your life in my hands from the moment we met together. If I had known.... It isn't that we can make you or guide you—I'm not pretending to be an inspiration—but—but we can release you. We needn't press upon you; we can save you from the instincts and passions that try to waste you altogether on us.... Yes, I'm beginning to understand. Oh, my child, my husband, my man! You talked of your wasted life!... I've been thinking—since first we left the Mersey. I've begun to see what it is to be a woman. For the first time in my life. We're the responsible sex. And we've forgotten it. We think we've done a wonder if we've borne men into the world and smiled a little, but indeed we've got to bear them all our lives.... A woman has to be steadier than a man and more self-sacrificing than a man, because when she plunges she does more harm than a man.... And what does she achieve if she does plunge? Nothing—nothing worth counting. Dresses and carpets and hangings and pretty arrangements, excitements and satisfactions and competition and more excitements. We can't do things. We don't bring things off! And you, you Monster! you Dream! you want to stick your hand out of all that is and make something that isn't, begin to be! That's the man——"

"Dear old Madge!" he said, "there's all sorts of women and all sorts of men."

"Well, our sort of women, then, and our sort of men."

"I doubt even that."

"I don't. I've found my place. I've been making my master my servant. We women— we've been looting all the good things in the world, and helping nothing. You've carried me on your back until you are loathing life. I've been making you fetch and carry for me, love me, dress me, keep me and my children, minister to my vanities and greeds.... No; let me go on. I'm so penitent, my dear, so penitent I want to kneel down here and marry you all over again, heal up your broken life and begin again."...

She paused.

"One doesn't begin again," she said. "But I want to take a new turn. Dear, you're still only a young man; we've thirty or forty years before us—forty years perhaps or more.... What shall we do with our years? We've loved, we've got children. What remains? Here we can plan it out, work it out, day after day. What shall we do with our lives and life? Tell me, make me your partner; it's you who know, what are we doing with life?"

§ 13

What are we doing with life?

That question overtakes a reluctant and fugitive humanity. The Traffords were but two of a great scattered host of people, who, obeying all the urgencies of need and desire, struggling, loving, begetting, enjoying, do nevertheless find themselves at last unsatisfied. They have lived the round of experience, achieved all that living creatures have sought since the beginning of the world—security and gratification and offspring—and they find themselves still strong, unsatiated, with power in their hands and years before them, empty of purpose. What are they to do?

The world presents such a spectacle of evasion as it has never seen before. Never was there such a boiling over and waste of vital energy. The Sphinx of our opportunity calls for the uttermost powers of heart and brain to read its riddle—the new, astonishing riddle of excessive power. A few give themselves to those honourable adventures that extend the range of man, they explore untravelled countries, climb remote mountains, conduct researches, risk life and limb in the fantastic experiments of flight, and a monstrous outpouring of labour and material goes on in the strenuous preparation for needless and improbable wars. The rest divert themselves with the dwarfish satisfactions of recognized vice, the meagre routine of pleasure, or still more timidly with sport and games—those new unscheduled perversions of the soul.

We are afraid of our new selves. The dawn of human opportunity appals us. Few of us dare look upon this strange light of freedom and limitless resources that breaks upon our world.

"Think," said Trafford, "while we sit here in this dark hut—think of the surplus life that wastes itself in the world for sheer lack of direction. Away there in England—I suppose that is westward"—he pointed—"there are thousands of men going out to-day to shoot. Think of the beautifully made guns, the perfected ammunition, the excellent clothes, the army of beaters, the carefully preserved woodland, the admirable science of it—all for that idiot massacre of half-tame birds! Just because man once had need to be a hunter! Think of the others again—golfing. Think of the big, elaborate houses from which they come, the furnishings, the service. And the women—dressing! Perpetually dressing. You, Marjorie—you've done nothing but dress since we married. No, let me abuse you, dear! It's insane, you know! You dress your minds a little to talk amusingly, you spread your minds out to backgrounds, to households, picturesque and delightful gardens, nurseries. Those nurseries! Think of our tremendously cherished and educated children! And when they grow up, what have we got for them? A feast of futility...."

§ 14

On the evening of the day when Trafford first tried to stand upon his leg, they talked far into the night. It had been a great and eventful day for them, full of laughter and exultation. He had been at first ridiculously afraid; he had clung to her almost childishly, and she had held him about the body with his weight on her strong right arm and his right arm in her left hand, concealing her own dread of a collapse under a mask of taunting courage. The crutch had proved admirable. "It's my silly knees!" Trafford kept on saying. "The leg's all right, but I get put out by my silly knees."

They made the day a feast, a dinner of two whole day's rations and a special soup instead of supper. "The birds will come," they explained to each other, "ducks and geese, long before May. May, you know, is the latest."

Marjorie confessed the habit of sharing his pipe was growing on her. "What shall we do in Tyburnia!" she said, and left it to the imagination.

"If ever we get back there," he said.

"I don't much fancy kicking a skirt before my shins again—and I'll be a black, coarse woman down to my neck at dinner for years to come!..."

Then, as he lay back in his bunk and she crammed the stove with fresh boughs and twigs of balsam that filled the little space about them with warmth and with a faint, sweet smell of burning and with flitting red reflections, he took up a talk about religion they had begun some days before.

"You see," he said, "I've always believed in Salvation. I suppose a man's shy of saying so—even to his wife. But I've always believed more or less distinctly that there was something up to which a life worked—always. It's been rather vague, I'll admit. I don't think I've ever believed in individual salvation. You see, I feel these are deep things, and the deeper one gets the less individual one becomes. That's why one thinks of those things in darkness and loneliness—and finds them hard to tell. One has an individual voice, or an individual birthmark, or an individualized old hat, but the soul— the soul's different.... It isn't me talking to you when it comes to that.... This question of what we are doing with life isn't a question to begin with for you and me as ourselves, but for you and me as mankind. Am I spinning it too fine, Madge?"

"No," she said, intent; "go on."

"You see, when we talk rations here, Marjorie, it's ourselves, but when we talk religion—it's mankind. You've either got to be Everyman in religion or leave it alone. That's my idea. It's no more presumptuous to think for the race than it is for a beggar to pray—though that means going right up to God and talking to Him. Salvation's a collective thing and a mystical thing—or there isn't any. Fancy the Almighty and me sitting up and keeping Eternity together! God and R. A. G. Trafford, F.R.S.—that's silly. Fancy a man in number seven boots, and a tailor-made suit in the nineteen-fourteen fashion, sitting before God! That's caricature. But God and Man! That's sense, Marjorie."...

He stopped and stared at her.

Marjorie sat red-lit, regarding him. "Queer things you say!" she said. "So much of this I've never thought out. I wonder why I've never done so.... Too busy with many things, I suppose. But go on and tell me more of these secrets you've kept from me!"

"Well, we've got to talk of these things as mankind—or just leave them alone, and shoot pheasants."...

"If I could shoot a pheasant now!" whispered Marjorie, involuntarily.

"And where do we stand? What do we need—I mean the whole race of us—kings and beggars together? You know, Marjorie, it's this,—it's Understanding. That's what mankind has got to, the realization that it doesn't understand, that it can't express, that it's purblind. We haven't got eyes for those greater things, but we've got the promise—the intimation of eyes. We've come out of an unsuspecting darkness, brute animal darkness, not into sight, that's been the mistake, but into a feeling of illumination, into a feeling of light shining through our opacity....

"I feel that man has now before all things to know. That's his supreme duty, to feel, realize, see, understand, express himself to the utmost limits of his power."

He sat up, speaking very earnestly to her, and in that flickering light she realized for the first time how thin he had become, how bright and hollow his eyes, his hair was long over his eyes, and a rough beard flowed down to his chest. "All the religions," he said, "all the philosophies, have pretended to achieve too much. We've no language yet for religious truth or metaphysical truth; we've no basis yet broad enough and strong enough on which to build. Religion and philosophy have been impudent and quackish—quackish! They've been like the doctors, who have always pretended they could cure since the beginning of things, cure everything, and to this day even they haven't got more than the beginnings of knowledge on which to base a cure. They've lacked humility, they've lacked the honour to say they didn't know; the priests took things of wood and stone, the philosophers took little odd arrangements of poor battered words, metaphors, analogies, abstractions, and said: "That's it! Think of their silly old Absolute,—ab-solutus, an untied parcel. I heard Haldane at the Aristotelian once, go on for an hour—no! it was longer than an hour—as glib and slick as a well-oiled sausage-machine, about the different sorts of Absolute, and not a soul of us laughed out at him! The vanity of such profundities! They've no faith, faith in patience, faith to wait for the coming of God. And since we don't know God, since we don't know His will with us, isn't it plain that all our lives should be a search for Him and it? Can anything else matter,—after we are free from necessity? That is the work now that is before all mankind, to attempt understanding—by the perpetual finding of thought and the means of expression, by perpetual extension and refinement of science, by the research that every artist makes for beauty and significance in his art, by the perpetual testing and destruction and rebirth under criticism of all these things, and by a perpetual extension of this intensifying wisdom to more minds and more minds and more, till all men share in it, and share in the making of it.... There you have my creed, Marjorie; there you have the very marrow of me."...

He became silent.

"Will you go back to your work?" she said, abruptly. "Go back to your laboratory?"

He stared at her for a moment without speaking. "Never," he said at last.

"But," she said, and the word dropped from her like a stone that falls down a well....

"My dear," he said, at last, "I've thought of that. But since I left that dear, dusty little laboratory, and all those exquisite subtle things—I've lived. I've left that man seven long years behind me. Some other man must go on—I think some younger man—with the riddles I found to work on then. I've grown—into something different. It isn't how atoms swing with one another, or why they build themselves up so and not so, that matters any more to me. I've got you and all the world in which we live, and a new set of riddles filling my mind, how thought swings about thought, how one man attracts his fellows, how the waves of motive and conviction sweep through a crowd and all the little drifting crystallizations of spirit with spirit and all the repulsions and eddies and difficulties, that one can catch in that turbulent confusion. I want to do a new sort of work now altogether.... Life has swamped me once, but I don't think it will get me under again;—I want to study men."

He paused and she waited, with a face aglow.

"I want to go back to watch and think—and I suppose write. I believe I shall write criticism. But everything that matters is criticism!... I want to get into contact with the men who are thinking. I don't mean to meet them necessarily, but to get into the souls of their books. Every writer who has anything to say, every artist who matters, is the stronger for every man or woman who responds to him. That's the great work—the Reality. I want to become a part of this stuttering attempt to express, I want at least to resonate, even if I do not help.... And you with me, Marjorie—you with me! Everything I write I want you to see and think about. I want you to read as I read.... Now after so long, now that, now that we've begun to talk, you know, talk again——"

Something stopped his voice. Something choked them both into silence. He held out a lean hand, and she shuffled on her knees to take it....

"Don't please make me," she stumbled through her thoughts, "one of those little parasitic, parroting wives—don't pretend too much about me—because you want me with you——. Don't forget a woman isn't a man."

"Old Madge," he said, "you and I have got to march together. Didn't I love you from the first, from that time when I was a boy examiner and you were a candidate girl—because your mind was clear?"

"And we will go back," she whispered, "with a work——"

"With a purpose," he said.

She disengaged herself from his arm, and sat close to him upon the floor. "I think I can see what you will do," she said. She mused. "For the first time I begin to see things as they may be for us. I begin to see a life ahead. For the very first time."

Queer ideas came drifting into her head. Suddenly she cried out sharply in that high note he loved. "Good heavens!" she said. "The absurdity! The infinite absurdity!"

"But what?"

"I might have married Will Magnet——. That's all."

She sprang to her feet. There came a sound of wind outside, a shifting of snow on the roof, and the door creaked. "Half-past eleven," she exclaimed looking at the watch that hung in the light of the stove door. "I don't want to sleep yet; do you? I'm going to brew some tea—make a convivial drink. And then we will go on talking. It's so good talking to you. So good!... I've an idea! Don't you think on this special day, it might run to a biscuit?" Her face was keenly anxious. He nodded. "One biscuit each," she said, trying to rob her voice of any note of criminality. "Just one, you know, won't matter."

She hovered for some moments close to the stove before she went into the arctic corner that contained the tin of tea. "If we can really live like that!" she said. "When we are home again."

"Why not?" he answered.

She made no answer, but went across for the tea....

He turned his head at the sound of the biscuit tin and watched her put out the precious discs.

"I shall have another pipe," he proclaimed, with an agreeable note of excess. "Thank heaven for unstinted tobacco...."

And now Marjorie's mind was teaming with thoughts of this new conception of a life lived for understanding. As she went about the preparation of the tea, her vividly concrete imagination was active with the realization of the life they would lead on their return. She could not see it otherwise than framed in a tall, fine room, a study, a study in sombre tones, with high, narrow, tall, dignified bookshelves and rich deep green curtains veiling its windows. There should be a fireplace of white marble, very plain and well proportioned, with furnishings of old brass, and a big desk towards the window beautifully lit by electric light, with abundant space for papers to lie. And she wanted some touch of the wilderness about it; a skin perhaps....

The tea was still infusing when she had determined upon an enormous paper-weight of that iridescent Labradorite that had been so astonishing a feature of the Green River Valley. She would have it polished on one side only—the other should be rough to show the felspar in its natural state....

It wasn't that she didn't feel and understand quite fully the intention and significance of all he had said, but that in these symbols of texture and equipment her mind quite naturally clothed itself. And while this room was coming into anticipatory being in her mind, she was making the tea very deftly and listening to Trafford's every word.

<h1 style="text-align:center">§ 15</h1>

That talk marked an epoch to Marjorie. From that day forth her imagination began to shape a new, ordered and purposeful life for Trafford and herself in London, a life not altogether divorced from their former life, but with a faith sustaining it and aims controlling it. She had always known of the breadth and power of his mind, but now as he talked of what he might do, what interests might converge and give results through him, it seemed she really knew him for the first time. In his former researches, so technical and withdrawn, she had seen little of his mind in action: now he was dealing in his own fashion with things she could clearly understand. There were times when his talk affected her like that joy of light one has in emerging into sunshine from a long and tedious cave. He swept things together, flashed unsuspected correlations upon her intelligence, smashed and scattered absurd yet venerated conventions of thought, made undreamt-of courses of action visible in a flare of luminous necessity. And she could follow him and help him. Just as she had hampered him and crippled him, so now she could release him—she fondled that word. She found a preposterous image in her mind that she hid like a disgraceful secret, that she tried to forget, and yet its stupendous, its dreamlike absurdity had something in it that shaped her delight as nothing else could do; she was, she told herself—hawking with an archangel!...

These were her moods of exaltation. And she was sure she had never loved her man before, that this was indeed her beginning. It was as if she had just found him....

Perhaps, she thought, true lovers keep on finding each other all through their lives.

And he too had discovered her. All the host of Marjories he had known, the shining, delightful, seductive, wilful, perplexing aspects that had so filled her life, gave place altogether for a time to this steady-eyed woman, lean and warm-wrapped with the valiant heart and the frost-roughened skin. What a fine, strong, ruddy thing she was! How glad he was for this wild adventure in the wilderness, if only because it had made him lie among the rocks and think of her and wait for her and despair of her life and God, and at last see her coming back to him, flushed with effort and calling his name to him out of that whirlwind of snow.... And there was at least one old memory mixed up with all these new and overmastering impressions, the memory of her clear unhesitating voice as it had stabbed into his life again long years ago, minute and bright in the telephone: "It's me, you know. It's Marjorie!"

Perhaps after all she had not wasted a moment of his life, perhaps every issue between them had been necessary, and it was good altogether to be turned from the study of crystals to the study of men and women....

And now both their minds were Londonward, where all the tides and driftage and currents of human thought still meet and swirl together. They were full of what they would do when they got back. Marjorie sketched that study to him—in general terms and without the paper-weight—and began to shape the world she would have about it. She meant to be his squaw and body-servant first of all, and then—a mother. Children, she said, are none the worse for being kept a little out of focus. And he was rapidly planning out his approach to the new questions to which he was now to devote his life. "One wants something to hold the work together," he said, and projected a book. "One cannot struggle at large for plain statement and copious and free and courageous statement, one needs a positive attack."

He designed a book, which he might write if only for the definition it would give him and with no ultimate publication, which was to be called: "The Limits of Language as a Means of Expression." ... It was to be a pragmatist essay, a sustained attempt to undermine the confidence of all that scholasticism and logic chopping which still lingers like the sequelæ of a disease in our University philosophy. "Those duffers sit in their studies and make a sort of tea of dry old words—and think they're distilling the spirit of wisdom," he said.

He proliferated titles for a time, and settled at last on "From Realism to Reality." He wanted to get at that at once; it fretted him to have to hang in the air, day by day, for want of books to quote and opponents to lance and confute. And he wanted to see pictures, too and plays, read novels he had heard of and never read, in order to verify or correct the ideas that were seething in his mind about the qualities of artistic expression. His thought had come out to a conviction that the line to wider human understandings lies through a huge criticism and cleaning up of the existing methods of formulation, as a preliminary to the wider and freer discussion of those religious and social issues our generation still shrinks from. "It's grotesque," he said, "and utterly true that the sanity and happiness of all the world lies in its habits of generalization." There was not even paper for him to make notes or provisional drafts of the new work. He hobbled about the camp fretting at these deprivations.

"Marjorie," he said, "we've done our job. Why should we wait here on this frosty shelf outside the world? My leg's getting sounder—if it wasn't for that feeling of ice in it.

Why shouldn't we make another sledge from the other bunk and start down—"

"To Hammond?"

"Why not?"

"But the way?"

"The valley would guide us. We could do four hours a day before we had to camp. I'm not sure we couldn't try the river. We could drag and carry all our food...."

She looked down the wide stretches of the valley. There was the hill they had christened Marjorie Ridge. At least it was familiar. Every night before nightfall if they started there would be a fresh camping place to seek among the snow-drifts, a great heap of wood to cut to last the night. Suppose his leg gave out—when they were already some days away, so that he could no longer go on or she drag him back to the stores. Plainly there would be nothing for it then but to lie down and die together....

And a sort of weariness had come to her as a consequence of two months of half-starved days, not perhaps a failure so much as a reluctance of spirit.

"Of course," she said, with a new aspect drifting before her mind, "then—we could eat. We could feed up before we started. We could feast almost!"

§ 16

"While you were asleep the other night," Trafford began one day as they sat spinning out their mid-day meal, "I was thinking how badly I had expressed myself when I talked to you the other day, and what a queer, thin affair I made of the plans I wanted to carry out. As a matter of fact, they're neither queer nor thin, but they are unreal in comparison with the common things of everyday life, hunger, anger, all the immediate desires. They must be. They only begin when those others are at peace. It's hard to set out these things; they're complicated and subtle, and one cannot simplify without falsehood. I don't want to simplify. The world has gone out of its way time after time through simplifications and short cuts. Save us from epigrams! And when one thinks over what one has said, at a little distance,—one wants to go back to it, and say it all again. I seem to be not so much thinking things out as reviving and developing things I've had growing in my mind ever since we met. It's as though an immense reservoir of thought had filled up in my mind at last and was beginning to trickle over and break down the embankment between us. This conflict that has been going on between our life together and my—my intellectual life; it's only just growing clear in my own mind. Yet it's just as if one turned up a light on something that had always been there....

"It's a most extraordinary thing to think out, Marjorie, that antagonism. Our love has kept us so close together and always our purposes have been—like that." He spread divergent hands. "I've speculated again and again whether there isn't something incurably antagonistic between women (that's you generalized, Marjorie) and men (that's me) directly we pass beyond the conditions of the individualistic struggle. I believe every couple of lovers who've ever married have felt that strain. Yet it's not a difference in kind between us but degree. The big conflict between us has a parallel in a little internal conflict that goes on; there's something of man in every woman and a touch of the feminine in every man. But you're nearer as woman to the immediate personal life of sense and reality than I am as man. It's been so ever since the men went hunting and fighting and the women kept hut, tended the children and gathered roots in the little cultivation close at hand. It's been so perhaps since the female carried and suckled her child and distinguished one male from another. It may be it will always be so. Men were released from that close, continuous touch with physical necessities long before women were. It's only now that women begin to be released. For ages now men have been wandering from field and home and city, over the hills and far away, in search of adventures and fresh ideas and the wells of mystery beyond the edge of the world, but it's only now that the woman comes with them too. Our difference isn't a difference in kind, old Marjorie; it's the difference between the old adventurer and the new feet upon the trail."

"We've got to come," said Marjorie.

"Oh! you've got to come. No good to be pioneers if the race does not follow. The women are the backbone of the race; the men are just the individuals. Into this Labrador and into all the wild and desolate places of thought and desire, if men come you women have to come too—and bring the race with you. Some day."

"A long day, mate of my heart."

"Who knows how long or how far? Aren't you at any rate here, dear woman of mine.... (Surely you are here)."

He went off at a tangent. "There's all those words that seem to mean something and then don't seem to mean anything, that keep shifting to and fro from the deepest significance to the shallowest of claptrap, Socialism, Christianity.... You know,—they aren't anything really, as yet; they are something trying to be.... Haven't I said that before, Marjorie?"

She looked round at him. "You said something like that when you were delirious," she answered, after a little pause. "It's one of the ideas that you're struggling with. You go on, old man, and talk. We've months—for repetitions."

"Well, I mean that all these things are seeking after a sort of co-operation that's greater than our power even of imaginative realization; that's what I mean. The kingdom of Heaven, the communion of saints, the fellowship of men; these are things like high peaks far out of the common life of every day, shining things that madden certain sorts of men to climb. Certain sorts of us! I'm a religious man, I'm a socialistic man. These calls are more to me than my daily bread. I've got something in me more generalizing than most men. I'm more so than many other men and most other women, I'm more socialistic than you...."

"You know, Marjorie, I've always felt you're a finer individual than me, I've never had a doubt of it. You're more beautiful by far than I, woman for my man. You've a keener appetite for things, a firmer grip on the substance of life. I love to see you do things, love to see you move, love to watch your hands; you've cleverer hands than mine by far.... And yet—I'm a deeper and bigger thing than you. I reach up to something you don't reach up to.... You're in life—and I'm a little out of it, I'm like one of those fish that began to be amphibian, I go out into something where you don't follow—where you hardly begin to follow.

"That's the real perplexity between thousands of men and women....

"It seems to me that the primitive socialism of Christianity and all the stuff of modern socialism that matters is really aiming—almost unconsciously, I admit at times—at one simple end, at the release of the human spirit from the individualistic struggle——

"You used 'release' the other day, Marjorie? Of course, I remember. It's queer how I go on talking after you have understood."

"It was just a flash," said Marjorie. "We have intimations. Neither of us really understands. We're like people climbing a mountain in a mist, that thins out for a moment and shows valleys and cities, and then closes in again, before we can recognize them or make out where we are."

Trafford thought. "When I talk to you, I've always felt I mustn't be too vague. And the very essence of all this is a vague thing, something we shall never come nearer to it in all our lives than to see it as a shadow and a glittering that escapes again into a mist.... And yet it's everything that matters, everything, the only thing that matters truly and for ever through the whole range of life. And we have to serve it with the keenest thought, the utmost patience, inordinate veracity....

"The practical trouble between your sort and my sort, Marjorie, is the trouble between faith and realization. You demand the outcome. Oh! and I hate to turn aside and realize. I've had to do it for seven years. Damnable years! Men of my sort want to understand. We want to understand, and you ask us to make. We want to understand atoms, ions, molecules, refractions. You ask us to make rubber and diamonds. I suppose it's right that incidentally we should make rubber and diamonds. Finally, I warn you, we will make rubber unnecessary and diamonds valueless. And again we want to understand how people react upon one another to produce social consequences, and you ask us to put it at once into a draft bill for the reform of something or other. I suppose life lies between us somewhere, we're the two poles of truth seeking and truth getting; with me alone it would be nothing but a luminous dream, with you nothing but a scramble in which sooner or later all the lamps would be upset.... But it's ever too much of a scramble yet, and ever too little of a dream. All our world over there is full of the confusion and wreckage of premature realizations. There's no real faith in thought and knowledge yet. Old necessity has driven men so hard that they still rush with a wild urgency—though she goads no more. Greed and haste, and if, indeed, we seem to have a moment's breathing space, then the Gawdsaker tramples us under."

"My dear!" cried Marjorie, with a sharp note of amusement. "What is a Gawdsaker?"

"Oh," said Trafford, "haven't you heard that before? He's the person who gets excited by any deliberate discussion and gets up wringing his hands and screaming, 'For Gawd's sake, let's do something now!' I think they used it first for Pethick Lawrence, that man who did so much to run the old militant suffragettes and burke the proper discussion of woman's future. You know. You used to have 'em in Chelsea—with their hats. Oh! 'Gawdsaking' is the curse of all progress, the hectic consumption that kills a thousand good beginnings. You see it in small things and in great. You see it in my life;

Gawdsaking turned my life-work to cash and promotions, Gawdsaking——Look at the way the aviators took to flying for prizes and gate-money, the way pure research is swamped by endowments for technical applications! Then that poor ghost-giant of an idea the socialists have;—it's been treated like one of those unborn lambs they kill for the fine skin of it, made into results before ever it was alive. Was there anything more pitiful? The first great dream and then the last phase! when your Aunt Plessington and the district visitors took and used it as a synonym for Payment in Kind.... It's natural, I suppose, for people to be eager for results, personal and immediate results—the last lesson of life is patience. Naturally they want reality, naturally! They want the individual life, something to handle and feel and use and live by, something of their very own before they die, and they want it now. But the thing that matters for the race, Marjorie, is a very different thing; it is to get the emerging thought process clear and to keep it clear—and to let those other hungers go. We've got to go back to England on the side of that delay, that arrest of interruption, that detached, observant, synthesizing process of the mind, that solvent of difficulties and obsolescent institutions, which is the reality of collective human life. We've got to go back on the side of pure science—literature untrammeled by the preconceptions of the social schemers—art free from the urgency of immediate utility—and a new, a regal, a god-like sincerity in philosophy. And, above all, we've got to stop this Jackdaw buying of yours, my dear, which is the essence of all that is wrong with the world, this snatching at everything, which loses everything worth having in life, this greedy confused realization of our accumulated resources! You're going to be a non-shopping woman now. You're to come out of Bond Street, you and your kind, like Israel leaving the Egyptian flesh-pots. You're going to be my wife and my mate.... Less of this service of things. Investments in comfort, in security, in experience, yes; but not just spending any more...."

He broke off abruptly with: "I want to go back and begin."

"Yes," said Marjorie, "we will go back," and saw minutely and distantly, and yet as clearly and brightly as if she looked into a concave mirror, that tall and dignified study, a very high room indeed, with a man writing before a fine, long-curtained window and a great lump of rich-glowing Labradorite upon his desk before him holding together an accumulation of written sheets....

She knew exactly the shop in Oxford Street where the stuff for the curtains might be best obtained.

17

One night Marjorie had been sitting musing before the stove for a long time, and suddenly she said: "I wonder if we shall fail. I wonder if we shall get into a mess again when we are back in London.... As big a mess and as utter a discontent as sent us here...."

Trafford was scraping out his pipe, and did not answer for some moments. Then he remarked: "What nonsense!"

"But we shall," she said. "Everybody fails. To some extent, we are bound to fail. Because indeed nothing is clear; nothing is a clear issue.... You know—I'm just the old Marjorie really in spite of all these resolutions—the spendthrift, the restless, the eager. I'm a born snatcher and shopper. We're just the same people really."

"No," he said, after thought. "You're all Labrador older."

"I always have failed," she considered, "when it came to any special temptations, Rag. I can't stand not having a thing!"

He made no answer.

"And you're still the same old Rag, you know," she went on. "Who weakens into kindness if I cry. Who likes me well-dressed. Who couldn't endure to see me poor."

"Not a bit of it. No! I'm a very different Rag with a very different Marjorie. Yes indeed! Things—are graver. Why!—I'm lame for life—and I've a scar. The very look of things is changed...." He stared at her face and said: "You've hidden the looking-glass and you think I haven't noted it——"

"It keeps on healing," she interrupted. "And if it comes to that—where's my complexion?" She laughed. "These are just the superficial aspects of the case."

"Nothing ever heals completely," he said, answering her first sentence, "and nothing ever goes back to the exact place it held before. We are different, you sun-bitten, frost-bitten wife of mine."...

"Character is character," said Marjorie, coming back to her point. "Don't exaggerate conversion, dear. It's not a bit of good pretending we shan't fall away, both of us. Each in our own manner. We shall. We shall, old man. London is still a tempting and confusing place, and you can't alter people fundamentally, not even by half-freezing and half-starving them. You only alter people fundamentally by killing them and replacing them. I shall be extravagant again and forget again, try as I may, and you will work again and fall away again and forgive me again. You know——It's just as though we were each of us not one person, but a lot of persons, who sometimes meet and shout all together, and then disperse and forget and plot against each other...."

"Oh, things will happen again," said Trafford, in her pause. "But they will happen again with a difference—after this. With a difference. That's the good of it all.... We've found something here—that makes everything different.... We've found each other, too, dear wife."

She thought intently.

"I am afraid," she whispered.

"But what is there to be afraid of?"

"Myself."

She spoke after a little pause that seemed to hesitate. "At times I wish—oh, passionately!—that I could pray."

"Why don't you?"

"I don't believe enough—in that. I wish I did."

Trafford thought. "People are always so exacting about prayer," he said.

"Exacting."

"You want to pray—and you can't make terms for a thing you want. I used to think I could. I wanted God to come and demonstrate a bit.... It's no good, Madge.... If God chooses to be silent—you must pray to the silence. If he chooses to live in darkness, you must pray to the night...."

"Yes," said Marjorie, "I suppose one must."

She thought. "I suppose in the end one does," she said....

18

Mixed up with this entirely characteristic theology of theirs and their elaborate planning-out of a new life in London were other strands of thought. Queer memories of London and old times together would flash with a peculiar brightness across their

contemplation of the infinities and the needs of mankind. Out of nowhere, quite disconnectedly, would come the human, finite: "Do you remember——?"

Two things particularly pressed into their minds. One was the thought of their children, and I do not care to tell how often in the day now they calculated the time in England, and tried to guess to a half mile or so where those young people might be and what they might be doing. "The shops are bright for Christmas now," said Marjorie. "This year Dick was to have had his first fireworks. I wonder if he did. I wonder if he burnt his dear little funny stumps of fingers. I hope not."

"Oh, just a little," said Trafford. "I remember how a squib made my glove smoulder and singed me, and how my mother kissed me for taking it like a man. It was the best part of the adventure."

"Dick shall burn his fingers when his mother's home to kiss him. But spare his fingers now, Dadda...."

The other topic was food.

It was only after they had been doing it for a week or so that they remarked how steadily they gravitated to reminiscences, suggestions, descriptions and long discussions of eatables—sound, solid eatables. They told over the particulars of dinners they had imagined altogether forgotten; neither hosts nor conversations seemed to matter now in the slightest degree, but every item in the menu had its place. They nearly quarrelled one day about hors-d'œuvre. Trafford wanted to dwell on them when Marjorie was eager for the soup.

"It's niggling with food," said Marjorie.

"Oh, but there's no reason," said Trafford, "why you shouldn't take a lot of hors-d'œuvre. Three or four sardines, and potato salad and a big piece of smoked salmon, and some of that Norwegian herring, and so on, and keep the olives by you to pick at. It's a beginning."

"It's—it's immoral," said Marjorie, "that's what I feel. If one needs a whet to eat, one shouldn't eat. The proper beginning of a dinner is soup—good, hot, rich soup. Thick soup—with things in it, vegetables and meat and things. Bits of oxtail."

"Not peas."

"No, not peas. Pea-soup is tiresome. I never knew anything one tired of so soon. I wish we hadn't relied on it so much."

"Thick soup's all very well," said Trafford, "but how about that clear stuff they give you in the little pavement restaurants in Paris. You know—Croûte-au-pot, with lovely great crusts and big leeks and lettuce leaves and so on! Tremendous aroma of onions, and beautiful little beads of fat! And being a clear soup, you see what there is. That's— interesting. Twenty-five centimes, Marjorie. Lord! I'd give a guinea a plate for it. I'd give five pounds for one of those jolly white-metal tureens full—you know, full, with little drops all over the outside of it, and the ladle sticking out under the lid."

"Have you ever tasted turtle soup?"

"Rather. They give it you in the City. The fat's—ripping. But they're rather precious with it, you know. For my own part, I don't think soup should be doled out. I always liked the soup we used to get at the Harts'; but then they never give you enough, you know—not nearly enough."

"About a tablespoonful," said Marjorie. "It's mocking an appetite."

"Still there's things to follow," said Trafford....

They discussed the proper order of a dinner very carefully. They decided that sorbets and ices were not only unwholesome, but nasty. "In London," said Trafford, "one's taste gets—vitiated."...

They weighed the merits of French cookery, modern international cookery, and produced alternatives. Trafford became very eloquent about old English food. "Dinners," said Trafford, "should be feasting, not the mere satisfaction of a necessity. There should be—amplitude. I remember a recipe for a pie; I think it was in one of those books that man Lucas used to compile. If I remember rightly, it began with: 'Take a swine and hew it into gobbets.' Gobbets! That's something like a beginning. It was a big pie with tiers and tiers of things, and it kept it up all the way in that key.... And then what could be better than prime British-fed roast beef, reddish, just a shade on the side of underdone, and not too finely cut. Mutton can't touch it."

"Beef is the best," she said.

"Then our English cold meat again. What can equal it? Such stuff as they give in a good country inn, a huge joint of beef—you cut from it yourself, you know as much as you like—with mustard, pickles, celery, a tankard of stout, let us say. Pressed beef, such as they'll give you at the Reform, too, that's good eating for a man. With chutney, and then old cheese to follow. And boiled beef, with little carrots and turnips and a dumpling or so. Eh?"

"Of course," said Marjorie, "one must do justice to a well-chosen turkey, a fat turkey."

"Or a good goose, for the matter of that—with honest, well-thought-out stuffing. I like the little sausages round the dish of a turkey, too; like cherubs they are, round the feet of a Madonna.... There's much to be said for sausage, Marjorie. It concentrates."

Sausage led to Germany. "I'm not one of those patriots," he was saying presently, "who run down other countries by way of glorifying their own. While I was in Germany I tasted many good things. There's their Leberwurst; it's never bad, and, at its best, it's splendid. It's only a fool would reproach Germany with sausage. Devonshire black-pudding, of course, is the master of any Blutwurst, but there's all those others on the German side, Frankfurter, big reddish sausage stuff again with great crystalline lumps of white fat. And how well they cook their rich hashes, and the thick gravies they make. Curious, how much better the cooking of Teutonic peoples is than the cooking of the South Europeans! It's as if one needed a colder climate to brace a cook to his business. The Frenchman and the Italian trifle and stimulate. It's as if they'd never met a hungry man. No German would have thought of soufflé. Ugh! it's vicious eating. There's much that's fine, though, in Austria and Hungary. I wish I had travelled in Hungary. Do you remember how once or twice we've lunched at that Viennese place in Regent Street, and how they've given us stuffed Paprika, eh?"

"That was a good place. I remember there was stewed beef once with a lot of barley— such good barley!"

"Every country has its glories. One talks of the cookery of northern countries and then suddenly one thinks of curry, with lots of rice."

"And lots of chicken!"

"And lots of hot curry powder, very hot. And look at America! Here's a people who haven't any of them been out of Europe for centuries, and yet they have as different a table as you could well imagine. There's a kind of fish, planked shad, that they cook on resinous wood—roast it, I suppose. It's substantial, like nothing else in the world. And how good, too, with turkey are sweet potatoes. Then they have such a multitude of cereal things; stuff like their buckwheat cakes, all swimming in golden syrup. And Indian corn, again!"

"Of course, corn is being anglicized. I've often given you corn—latterly, before we came away."

"That sort of separated grain—out of tins. Like chicken's food! It's not the real thing. You should eat corn on the cob—American fashion! It's fine. I had it when I was in the States. You know, you take it up in your hands by both ends—you've seen the cobs?—and gnaw."

The craving air of Labrador at a temperature of -20° Fahrenheit, and methodically stinted rations, make great changes in the outward qualities of the mind. "I'd like to do that," said Marjorie.

Her face flushed a little at a guilty thought, her eyes sparkled. She leant forward and spoke in a confidential undertone.

"I'd—I'd like to eat a mutton chop like that," said Marjorie.

<h3 style="text-align:center">§ 20</h3>

One morning Marjorie broached something she had had on her mind for several days.

"Old man," she said, "I can't stand it any longer. I'm going to thaw my scissors and cut your hair.... And then you'll have to trim that beard of yours."

"You'll have to dig out that looking-glass."

"I know," said Marjorie. She looked at him. "You'll never be a pretty man again," she said. "But there's a sort of wild splendour.... And I love every inch and scrap of you...."

Their eyes met. "We're a thousand deeps now below the look of things," said Trafford. "We'd love each other minced."

She broke into that smiling laugh of hers. "Oh! it won't come to that," she said. "Trust my housekeeping!"

CHAPTER THE FIFTH

The Trail to the Sea

§ 1

One astonishing afternoon in January a man came out of the wilderness to Lonely Hut. He was a French-Indian half-breed, a trapper up and down the Green River and across the Height of Land to Sea Lake. He arrived in a sort of shy silence, and squatted amiably on a log to thaw. "Much snow," he said, "and little fur."

After he had sat at their fire for an hour and eaten and drunk, his purpose in coming thawed out. He explained he had just come on to them to see how they were. He was, he said, a planter furring; he had a line of traps, about a hundred and twenty miles in length. The nearest trap in his path before he turned northward over the divide was a good forty miles down the river. He had come on from there. Just to have a look. His name, he said, was Louis Napoleon Partington. He had carried a big pack, a rifle and a dead marten,—they lay beside him—and out of his shapeless mass of caribou skins and woolen clothing and wrappings, peeped a genial, oily, brown face, very dirty, with a strand of blue-black hair across one eye, irregular teeth in its friendly smile, and little, squeezed-up eyes.

Conversation developed. There had been doubts of his linguistic range at first, but he had an understanding expression, and his English seemed guttural rather than really bad.

He was told the tremendous story of Trafford's leg; was shown it, and felt it; he interpolated thick and whistling noises to show how completely he followed their explanations, and then suddenly he began a speech that made all his earlier taciturnity seem but the dam of a great reservoir of mixed and partly incomprehensible English. He complimented Marjorie so effusively and relentlessly and shamelessly as to produce a pause when he had done. "Yes," he said, and nodded to button up the whole. He sucked his pipe, well satisfied with his eloquence. Trafford spoke in his silence. "We are coming down," he said.

("I thought, perhaps——" whispered Louis Napoleon.)

"Yes," said Trafford, "we are coming down with you. Why not? We can get a sledge over the snow now? It's hard? I mean a flat sledge—like this. See? Like this." He got up and dragged Marjorie's old arrangement into view. "We shall bring all the stuff we can down with us, grub, blankets—not the tent, it's too bulky; we'll leave a lot of the heavy gear."

"You'd have to leave the tent," said Louis Napoleon.

"I said leave the tent."

"And you'd have to leave ... some of those tins."

"Nearly all of them."

"And the ammunition, there;—except just a little."

"Just enough for the journey down."

"Perhaps a gun?"

"No, not a gun. Though, after all,—well, we'd return one of the guns. Give it you to bring back here."

"Bring back here?"

"If you liked."

For some moments Louis Napoleon was intently silent. When he spoke his voice was guttural with

emotion. "After," he said thoughtfully and paused, and then resolved to have it over forthwith, "all you leave will be mine? Eh?"

Trafford said that was the idea.

Louis Napoleon's eye brightened, but his face preserved its Indian calm.

"I will take you right to Hammond's," he said, "Where they have dogs. And then I can come back here...."

They had talked out nearly every particular of their return before they slept that night; they yarned away three hours over the first generous meal that any one of them had eaten for many weeks. Louis Napoleon stayed in the hut as a matter of course, and reposed with snores and choking upon Marjorie's sledge and within a yard of her. It struck her as she lay awake and listened that the housemaids in Sussex Square would have thought things a little congested for a lady's bedroom, and then she reflected that after all it wasn't much worse than a crowded carriage in an all-night train from Switzerland. She tried to count how many people there had been in that compartment, and failed. How stuffy that had been—the smell of cheese and all! And with that, after a dream that she was whaling and had harpooned a particularly short-winded whale she fell very peacefully into oblivion.

Next day was spent in the careful preparation of the two sledges. They intended to take a full provision for six weeks, although they reckoned that with good weather they ought to be down at Hammond's in four.

The day after was Sunday, and Louis Napoleon would not look at the sledges or packing. Instead he held a kind of religious service which consisted partly in making Trafford read aloud out of a very oily old New Testament he produced, a selected passage from the book of Corinthians, and partly in moaning rather than singing several hymns. He was rather disappointed that they did not join in with him. In the afternoon he heated some water, went into the tent with it and it would appear partially washed his face. In the evening, after they had supped, he discussed religion, being curious by this time about their beliefs and procedure.

He spread his mental and spiritual equipment before them very artlessly. Their isolation and their immense concentration on each other had made them sensitive to personal quality, and they listened to the broken English and the queer tangential starts into new topics of this dirty mongrel creature with the keenest appreciation of its quality. It was inconsistent, miscellaneous, simple, honest, and human. It was as touching as the medley in the pocket of a dead schoolboy. He was superstitious and sceptical and sensual and spiritual, and very, very earnest. The things he believed, even if they were just beliefs about the weather or drying venison or filling pipes, he believed with emotion. He flushed as he told them. For all his intellectual muddle they felt he knew how to live honestly and die if need be very finely.

He was more than a little distressed at their apparent ignorance of the truths of revealed religion as it is taught in the Moravian schools upon the coast, and indeed it was manifest that he had had far more careful and infinitely more sincere religious teaching than either Trafford or Marjorie. For a time the missionary spirit inspired him, and then he quite forgot his solicitude for their conversion in a number of increasingly tall anecdotes about hunters and fishermen, illustrating at first the extreme dangers of any departure from a rigid Sabbatarianism, but presently becoming just stories illustrating the uncertainty of life. Thence he branched off to the general topic of life upon the coast and the relative advantages of "planter" and fisherman.

And then with a kindling eye he spoke of women, and how that some day he would marry. His voice softened, and he addressed himself more particularly to Marjorie. He didn't so much introduce the topic of the lady as allow the destined young woman suddenly to pervade his discourse. She was, it seemed, a servant, an Esquimaux girl at the Moravian Mission station at Manivikovik. He had been plighted to her for nine years. He described a gramophone he had purchased down at Port Dupré and brought back to her three hundred miles up the coast—it seemed to Marjorie an odd gift for an Esquimaux maiden—and he gave his views upon its mechanism. He said God was with the man who invented the gramophone "truly." They would have found one a very great relief to the tediums of their sojourn at Lonely Hut. The gramophone he had given his betrothed possessed records of the Rev. Capel Gumm's preaching and of Madame Melba's singing, a revival hymn called "Sowing the Seed," and a comic song— they could not make out his pronunciation of the title—that made you die with laughter. "It goes gobble, gobble, gobble," he said, with a solemn appreciative reflection of those distant joys.

"It's good to be jolly at times," he said with his bright eyes scanning Marjorie's face a little doubtfully, as if such ideas were better left for week-day expression.

§ 3

Their return was a very different journey from the toilsome ascent of the summer. An immense abundance of snow masked the world, snow that made them regret acutely they had not equipped themselves with ski. With ski and a good circulation, a man may go about Labrador in winter, six times more easily than by the canoes and slow trudging of summer travel. As it was they were glad of their Canadian snow shoes. One needs only shelters after the Alpine Club hut fashion, and all that vast solitary country would be open in the wintertime. Its shortest day is no shorter than the shortest day in

Cumberland or Dublin.

This is no place to tell of the beauty and wonder of snow and ice, the soft contours of gentle slopes, the rippling of fine snow under a steady wind, the long shadow ridges of shining powder on the lee of trees and stones and rocks, the delicate wind streaks over broad surfaces like the marks of a chisel in marble, the crests and cornices, the vivid brightness of edges in the sun, the glowing yellowish light on sunlit surfaces, the long blue shadows, the flush of sunset and sunrise and the pallid unearthly desolation of snow beneath the moon. Nor need the broken snow in woods and amidst tumbled stony slopes be described, nor the vast soft overhanging crests on every outstanding rock beside the icebound river, nor the huge stalactites and stalagmites of green-blue ice below the cliffs, nor trees burdened and broken by frost and snow, nor snow upon ice, nor the blue pools at mid-day upon the surface of the ice-stream. Across the smooth wind-swept ice of the open tarns they would find a growth of ice flowers, six-rayed and complicated, more abundant and more beautiful than the Alpine summer flowers.

But the wind was very bitter, and the sun had scarcely passed its zenith before the thought of fuel and shelter came back into their minds.

As they approached Partington's tilt, at the point where his trapping ground turned out of the Green River gorge, he became greatly obsessed by the thought of his traps. He began to talk of all that he might find in them, all he hoped to find, and the "dallars" that might ensue. They slept the third night, Marjorie within and the two men under the lee of the little cabin, and Partington was up and away before dawn to a trap towards the ridge. He had infected Marjorie and Trafford with a sympathetic keenness, but when they saw his killing of a marten that was still alive in its trap, they suddenly conceived a distaste for trapping.

They insisted they must witness no more. They would wait while he went to a trap....

"Think what he's doing!" said Trafford, as they sat together under the lee of a rock waiting for him. "We imagined this was a free, simple-souled man leading an unsophisticated life on the very edge of humanity, and really he is as much a dependant of your woman's world, Marjorie, as any sweated seamstress in a Marylebone slum. Lord! how far those pretty wasteful hands of women reach! All these poor broken and starving beasts he finds and slaughters are, from the point of view of our world, just furs. Furs! Poor little snarling unfortunates! Their pelts will be dressed and prepared because women who have never dreamt of this bleak wilderness desire them. They will get at last into Regent Street shops, and Bond Street shops, and shops in Fifth Avenue and in Paris and Berlin, they will make delightful deep muffs, with scent and little bags and powder puffs and all sorts of things tucked away inside, and long wraps for tall women, and jolly little frames of soft fur for pretty faces, and dainty coats and rugs for expensive little babies in Kensington Gardens."...

"I wonder," reflected Marjorie, "if I could buy one perhaps. As a memento."

He looked at her with eyes of quiet amusement.

"Oh!" she cried, "I didn't mean to! The old Eve!"

"The old Adam is with her," said Trafford. "He's wanting to give it her.... We don't cease to be human, Madge, you know, because we've got an idea now of just where we are. I wonder, which would you like? I dare say we could arrange it."

"No," said Marjorie, and thought. "It would be jolly," she said. "All the same, you know—and just to show you—I'm not going to let you buy me that fur."

"I'd like to," said Trafford.

"No," said Marjorie, with a decision that was almost fierce. "I mean it. I've got more to do than you in the way of reforming. It's just because always I've let my life be made up of such little things that I mustn't. Indeed I mustn't. Don't make things hard for me."

He looked at her for a moment. "Very well," he said. "But I'd have liked to."...

"You're right," he added, five seconds later.

"Oh! I'm right."

§ 4

One day Louis Napoleon sent them on along the trail while he went up the mountain to a trap among the trees. He rejoined them—not as his custom was, shouting inaudible conversation for the last hundred yards or so, but in silence. They wondered at that, and at the one clumsy gesture that flourished something darkly grey at them. What had happened to the man? Whatever he had caught he was hugging it as one hugs a cat, and stroking it. "Ugh!" he said deeply, drawing near. "Oh!" A solemn joy irradiated his face, and almost religious ecstasy found expression.

He had got a silver fox, a beautifully marked silver fox, the best luck of Labrador! One goes for years without one, in hope, and when it comes, it pays the trapper's debts, it clears his life—for years!

They tried poor inadequate congratulation....

As they sat about the fire that night a silence came upon Louis Napoleon. It was manifest that his mind was preoccupied. He got up, walked about, inspected the miracle of fur that had happened to him, returned, regarded them. "'M'm," he said, and stroked his chin with his forefinger. A certain diffidence and yet a certain dignity of assurance mingled in his manner. It wasn't so much a doubt of his own correctness as of some possible ignorance of the finer shades on their part that might embarrass him. He coughed a curt preface, and intimated he had a request to make. Behind the Indian calm of his face glowed tremendous feeling, like the light of a foundry furnace shining through chinks in the door. He spoke in a small flat voice, exercising great self-control. His wish, he said, in view of all that had happened, was a little thing.... This was nearly a perfect day for him, and one thing only remained.... "Well," he said, and hung. "Well," said Trafford. He plunged. Just simply this. Would they give him the brandy bottle and let him get drunk? Mr. Grenfell was a good man, a very good man, but he had made brandy dear—dear beyond the reach of common men altogether—along the coast....

He explained, dear bundle of clothes and dirt! that he was always perfectly respectable when he was drunk.

§ 5

It seemed strange to Trafford that now that Marjorie was going home, a wild impatience to see her children should possess her. So long as it had been probable that they would stay out their year in Labrador, that separation had seemed mainly a sentimental trouble; now at times it was like an animal craving. She would talk of them for hours at a stretch, and when she was not talking he could see her eyes fixed ahead, and knew that she was anticipating a meeting. And for the first time it seemed the idea of possible misadventure troubled her....

They reached Hammond's in one and twenty days from Lonely Hut, three days they had been forced to camp because of a blizzard, and three because Louis Napoleon was rigidly Sabbatarian. They parted from him reluctantly, and the next day Hammond's produced its dogs, twelve stout but extremely hungry dogs, and sent the Traffords on to the Green River pulp-mills, where there were good beds and a copious supply of hot water. Thence they went to Manivikovik, and thence the new Marconi station sent their inquiries home, inquiries that were answered next day with matter-of-fact brevity: "Everyone well, love from all."

When the operator hurried with that to Marjorie she received it off-handedly, glanced at it carelessly, asked him to smoke, remarked that wireless telegraphy was a wonderful thing, and then, in the midst of some unfinished commonplace about the temperature, broke down and wept wildly and uncontrollably....

§ 6

Then came the long, wonderful ride southward day after day along the coast to Port Dupré, a ride from headland to headland across the frozen bays behind long teams of straining, furry dogs, that leapt and yelped as they ran. Sometimes over the land the brutes shirked and loitered and called for the whip; they were a quarrelsome crew to keep waiting; but across the sea-ice they went like the wind, and downhill the komatic chased their waving tails. The sledges swayed and leapt depressions, and shot athwart icy stretches. The Traffords, spectacled and wrapped to their noses, had all the sensations then of hunting an unknown quarry behind a pack of wolves. The snow blazed under the sun, out to sea beyond the ice the water glittered, and it wasn't so much air they breathed as a sort of joyous hunger.

One day their teams insisted upon racing.

Marjorie's team was the heavier, her driver more skillful, and her sledge the lighter, and she led in that wild chase from start to finish, but ever and again Trafford made wild spurts that brought him almost level. Once, as he came alongside, she heard him laughing joyously.

"Marjorie," he shouted, "d'you remember? Old donkey cart?"

Her team yawed away, and as he swept near again, behind his pack of whimpering, straining, furious dogs, she heard him shouting, "You know, that old cart! Under the overhanging trees! So thick and green they met overhead! You know! When you and I had our first talk together! In the lane. It wasn't so fast as this, eh?"...

§ 7

At Port Dupré they stayed ten days—days that Marjorie could only make tolerable by knitting absurd garments for the children (her knitting was atrocious), and then one afternoon they heard the gun of the Grenfell, the new winter steamer from St. John's, signalling as it came in through the fog, very slowly, from that great wasteful world of men and women beyond the seaward grey.

THE END